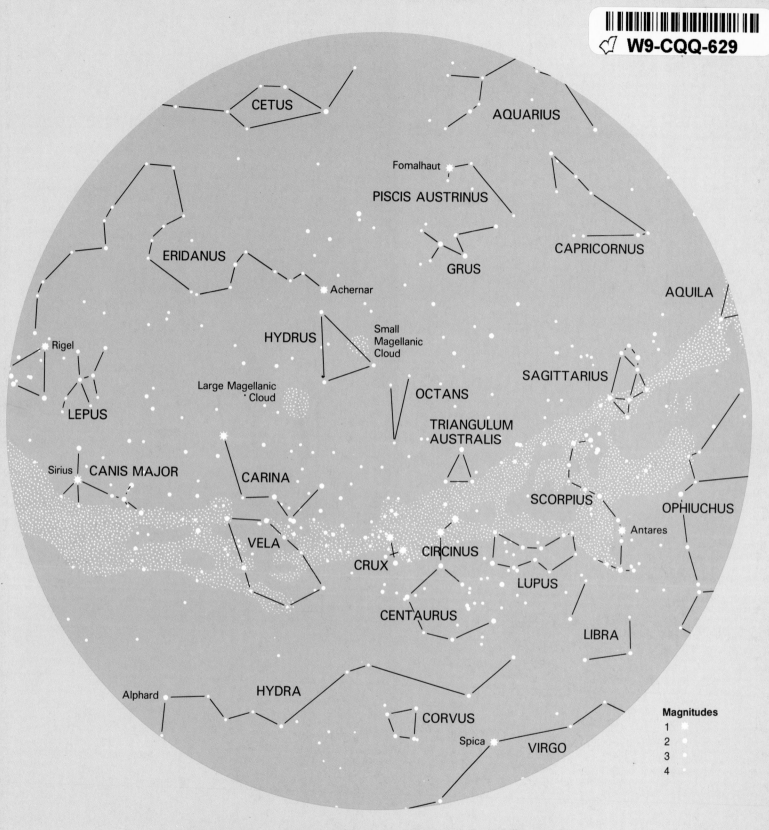

South Celestial Hemisphere

reaches its brightest in the southern sky. Two small galaxies, the Magellanic Clouds, appear near the south celestial pole. Companions of our Milky Way Galaxy, these small star clouds can be seen well only from southern latitudes.

Rand McNally
Children's Atlas of the
Universe

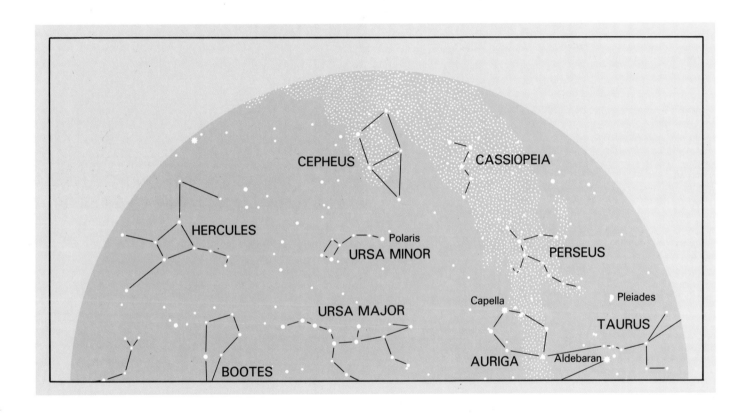

CEPHEUS

CASSIOPEIA

HERCULES

Polaris

URSA MINOR

PERSEUS

Pleiades

Capella

TAURUS

URSA MAJOR

AURIGA   Aldebaran

BOOTES

Rand McNally

Chicago • New York • San Francisco

Rand McNally Children's Atlas of the Universe

General manager: Russell L. Voisin
Managing editor: Jon M. Leverenz
Editor: Elizabeth G. Fagan
Writer: Francis Reddy
Designer: Corasue Nicholas
Production editor: Laura C. Schmidt
Production managers: John R. Potratz, Patricia Martin

Photograph and illustration credits: 8-9: McDonald Observatory/©Lee Ann Wilson; Chichen Itza/Francis Reddy; Preparing IRAS for launch/NASA; Apollo 17/NASA. 10-11: © 1989 Ron Miller/All rights reserved. 12-13: Earth/NASA 72-HC-928; Mt. St. Helens/R. Hoblitt/United States Geological Survey; San Andreas Fault/R.E. Wallace/United States Geological Survey. 14-15: Hurricane Elena/NASA; Lightning/Francis Reddy. 16-17: Plankton bloom/Dennis Clark; North America/U.S. Air Force Defense Meteorological Satellite Program. 18-19: Moonrise/NASA; Moon/NASA 88-H-372; Impact/© William Hartmann/All rights reserved. 20-21: Venus/NASA; Venus/United States Geological Survey. 22-23: Soviet lander on Venus/©1982 James Hervat; US superimposed over Venus/NASA; Venus surface/TASS/Sovfoto. 24-25: Mars mosaic/United States Geological Survey; Mars south pole/United States Geological Survey. 26-27: Mars mosaic closeup/United States Geological Survey; Viking shot of Mars/NASA; Mars landing/NASA; Phobos/NASA; Deimos/NASA. 28-29: Mercury mosaic/NASA; Mercury closeup/NASA. 30-31: Impact painting/© 1989 Ron Miller/All rights reserved; Crater/D.J. Roddy/United States Geological Survey. 32-33: Second largest meteorite/Neg. No. 45086/Photo by Orchard/Courtesy Department of Library Services/American Museum of Natural History; Asteroid/© William Hartmann/All rights reserved. 34-35: © 1989 Ron Miller/All rights reserved. 36-37: Moons over red spot/NASA/JPL; Earth superimposed over red spot/NASA. 38-39: Jupiter rings/NASA/JPL; Moons/NASA; Volcano on Io/© 1981 Ron Miller/All rights reserved. 40-41: Saturn/NASA/JPL; Computer image of Saturn/NASA/JPL. 44-45: Uranus/NASA/JPL; Uranus rings/NASA/JPL. 46-47: Umbriel/NASA/JPL; Titania/NASA/JPL; Miranda mosaic/NASA/JPL. 48-49: Neptune/NASA/JPL; Neptune closeup/NASA/JPL. 50-51: Triton closeup/JPL P-34719; Triton/NASA/JPL. 52-53: Pluto fly-by/© Ron Miller/All rights reserved; Charon eclipsing Pluto/Marc Buie/Space Telescope Science Institute. 54-55: Comet West/Ronald E. Royer and Steve Padilla; Ikeya-Seki/Alfred Lilge. 56-57: Meteors falling over Niagara Falls/Courtesy Griffith Observatory; Comet colliding with sun/Naval Research Laboratory; Comet surface/© William Hartmann; Halley's nucleus/Courtesy of Harold Reitsema and Alan Delamere/Ball Aerospace/© 1986 Max Planck/Istitut für Aeronomie. 58-59: © 1989 Ron Miller/All rights reserved. 60-61: Sun/National Solar Observatory; Sunspots/National Solar Observatory. 62-63: Solar flares/National Solar Observatory; Eclipse/National Solar Observatory. 64-65: Orion nebula/©1981 Anglo-Australian Telescope Board; Orion region/NASA. 66-67: Beta Pictoris/NASA/JPL; Beta Pictoris/from *Cycles of Fire* © 1987 by William Hartmann/Painting © Ron Miller/Used by permission of Workman Publishing/All rights reserved; Life cycle/© 1989 Ron Miller/All rights reserved. 68-69: Crab Nebula/© California Institute of Technology and Carnegie Institute of Washington; Ring Nebula/© California Institute of Technology and Carnegie Institute of Washington; Supernova/© California Institute of Technology and Carnegie Institute of Washington. 70-71: © 1989 Ron Miller/All rights reserved. 72-73: Milky Way/National Optical Astronomy Observatories; Lagoon Nebula/© Association of Universities for Research in Astronomy, Inc. 74-75: Galaxy cluster/National Optical Astronomy Observatories 4046; Galaxy cluster/National Optical Astronomy Observatories 4048; Galaxy/© 1989 Ron Miller/All rights reserved; Plan of galaxy/© 1989 Ron Miller/All rights reserved; Arms of galaxy/© 1989 Ron Miller/All rights reserved. 76-77: Galaxy in Andromeda/© Association of Universities for Research in Astronomy, Inc.; Galaxy in Dorado/© Association of Universities for Research in Astronomy, Inc.; Galaxy M87/National Optical Astronomy Observatories. 78-79: Galaxy in Triangulum/© Association of Universities for Research in Astronomy, Inc.; Galaxy/National Optical Astronomy Observatories 2208; Galaxy M51/© Dr. James Wray, from *The Color Atlas of Galaxies*, Cambridge University Press, 1988. 80-81: Galaxies/National Optical Astronomy Observatories 2300; Quasar/from *Cycles of Fire* © 1987 by William Hartmann/Painting ©Ron Miller/Used by permission of Workman Publishing/All rights reserved. 82-83: Betty Maxey. 84-85: Celestial sphere/© 1989 Ron Miller/All rights reserved.

Library of Congress Catalog Card Number: 90-52622
ISBN: 0-528-83408-8

Contents

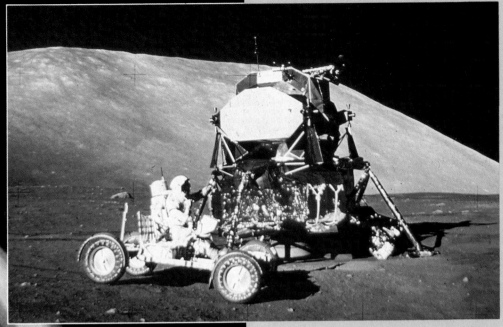

Left: The Maya people of ancient Mexico were great astronomers. They used this building, the Caracol of Chichen Itza, to study the planet Venus.

Bottom: Engineers prepare a satellite for its launch into space.

Right: In the 1970s, astronauts walked and drove on the Moon's surface.

Background: Stars silently wheel above the dome where a giant telescope awaits a glimpse of space. The stars look trailed because the Earth rotates, moving the camera and smearing the stars.

Exploring the Universe

Since ancient times, people have looked to the sky with wonder. Why, they asked, did the Sun arc each day through the heavens? Why did the Moon change shape throughout each month? What were the five "wandering stars" that seemed to move with a will of their own? People made up stories to explain what they saw.

The answers to such questions are now known. The Sun moves across the sky because the rotation of the planet Earth spins into the Sun's light. The Moon circles the Earth each month, and its cycle of changes shows its progress. Today it is known that the "wandering stars" are the brightest of eight other planets that, like the Earth, circle the nearby star called the Sun.

People are no longer content just to look at the night sky— they have moved out into it. The telescope, invented nearly four hundred years ago, allowed early astronomers to explore space. Since then, astronomers have built telescopes that see into the farthest regions of the universe. Robot spacecraft have visited all but one of the other planets. And in a true step into space, astronauts have even walked on the surface of the Moon.

This book explores the strange new worlds of the universe. Read about distant planets, watch the birth and death of stars, leave the galaxy, and view the most distant things astronomers know about.

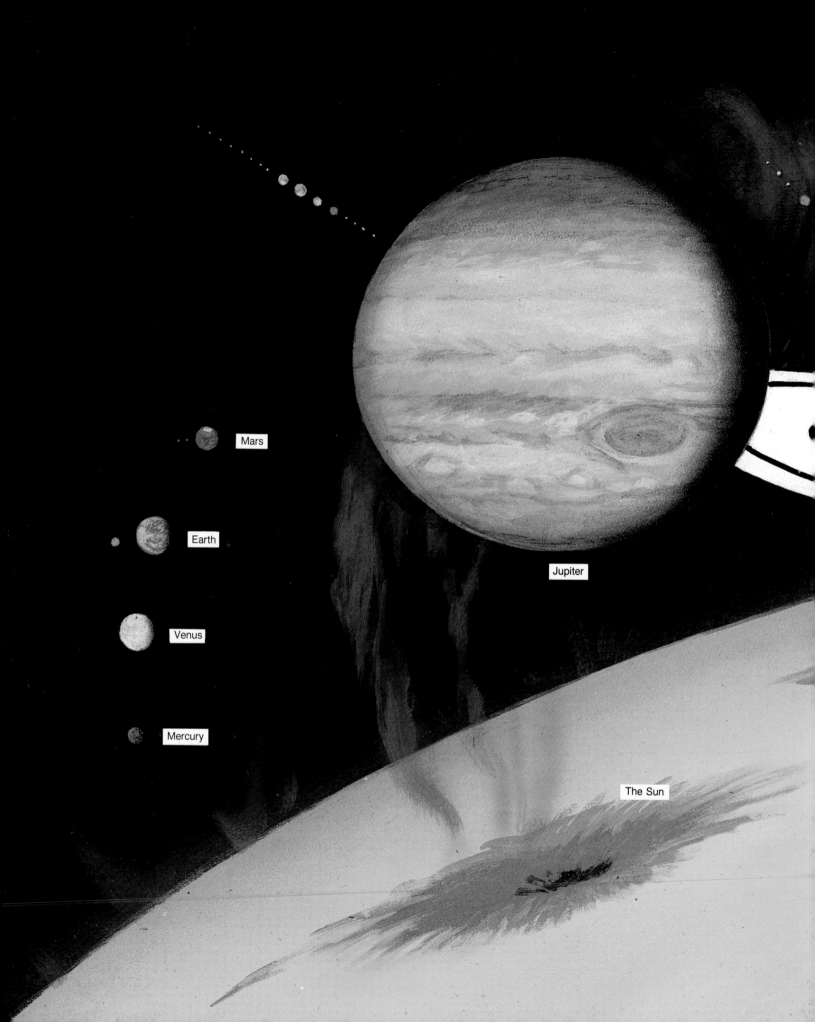

Pluto

Neptune

Uranus

Saturn

The Realm of the Earth

When placed beside the other planets in the solar system, Earth can be a little hard to find. This portrait shows the solar system's planets and moons at the same scale. The flaming arc at the bottom is all of the Sun that fits into the picture.

A Visit to Our Home Planet

A World of Rock

Planet Earth is special in many ways. As this book takes a journey through space, it will compare the strange new landscapes to more familiar sights here on Earth. First we will take a close look at our home planet.

Of the small rocky planets that orbit close to the Sun, Earth is the largest. Its surface, a wrinkled layer of solid rock called the *crust*, is between five and twenty miles (ten and thirty-two kilometers) thick. The Earth's oceans fill the crust's deepest basins, taking up about two-thirds of the surface. Humans occupy the highest areas on the planet—the seven continents of Africa, North and South America, Asia, Australia, Europe, and barren, ice-covered Antarctica.

Unlike any other planet, Earth's surface constantly changes. The crust is cracked into a dozen separate plates that move around. Beneath the crust, where temperatures rise above 1,700° F (900° C), rock turns into a thick liquid. As molten rock moves under the crust, it pushes the surface plates against one another. Earthquakes occur when one plate suddenly slips against another. Where molten rock reaches the surface, volcanoes erupt with fountains of lava. Mountains build from the slow collision of Earth's rocky plates.

Other worlds have their own spectacles, but only Earth has a surface where rock seems so alive.

Earth's clouds swirl above the familiar outline of Africa (center) and mix with the icy glare of Antarctica's polar cap (bottom). Appreciating how truly special Earth is can only be done by visiting other worlds. The Earth's crust is broken into giant plates that bump and grind against each other. The slow movement of the Pacific and North American plates creates earthquakes and volcanoes along North America's west coast.

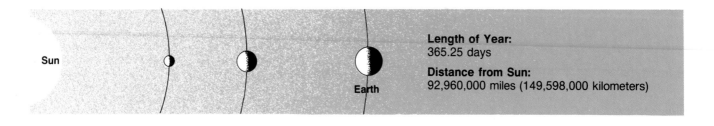

Sun

Earth

Length of Year:
365.25 days

Distance from Sun:
92,960,000 miles (149,598,000 kilometers)

North
American
Plate

Pacific Plate

Facts About Earth

Diameter:
7,926 miles (12,756 km)

Average Surface Temperature:
58° F (14° C)

Surface Pressure:
1 atmosphere

Atmosphere:
78% nitrogen, 21% oxygen

Length of Day:
23 hours, 56 minutes

Satellites:
1

Satellite Data

Name	Diameter
Moon	2,160 miles (3,476 km)

Along the San Andreas fault in California, two crustal plates (above) grind past one another. As the plates move, they split a stream that crosses the fault (below).

When one plate slides under another, molten rock works its way upward. A fresh source of molten rock reactivated Mount St. Helens in Washington State.

A World of Air

The hazards of space are never far. Chunks of rock large and small plunge toward Earth each day. Even the Sun threatens with ultraviolet light and dangerous particles that are harmful to humans.

A thin shell of gas called the *atmosphere,* made mostly from nitrogen (78 percent) and oxygen (21 percent), protects people from these dangers. If Earth were reduced to the size of an apple, this protective layer of gas would be as thin as an apple's skin.

Space debris usually burns up in the atmosphere. From about ten to thirty miles (fifteen to fifty kilometers) up, a gas called *ozone*

A collar of tall thunderclouds marks the central eye of Hurricane Elena, which roamed the Atlantic Ocean in 1985. Hurricanes are the most powerful storms on the planet. Spiral clouds trace air streaming into the storm center, where winds often reach speeds of over 110 miles (176 kilometers) an hour.

screens out most of the Sun's ultraviolet light. Hazardous particles from the Sun are stopped before they stream within sixty miles (about one hundred kilometers) of the surface. They create the beautiful lights called the *aurora* by striking high-altitude gas atoms and setting them aglow.

Humans live at the bottom of Earth's ocean of air in a region called the *troposphere*. All of the activity called *weather* occurs here. Between five and ten miles (eight and sixteen kilometers) thick, this bottom layer holds about 75 percent of the atmosphere's mass. Just a tiny fraction of the water on Earth's surface exists as a gas. But the properties of water vapor keep the troposphere constantly churning with ever-changing clouds and mighty storms.

Of all the planets in the solar system, only Earth has an atmosphere with the oxygen humans need to breathe. And this atmosphere creates an environment in which liquid water flows freely on Earth's surface. This happens nowhere else in the solar system.

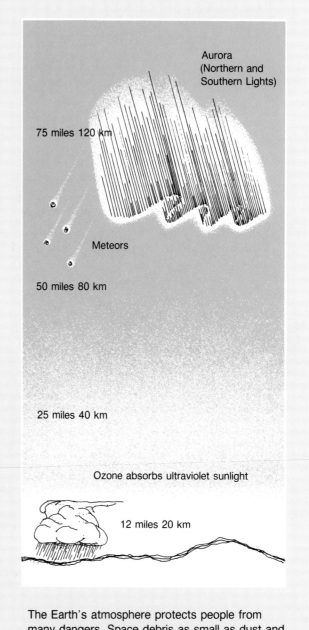

The Earth's atmosphere protects people from many dangers. Space debris as small as dust and as large as automobiles break up in the atmosphere, and are often visible as shooting stars, or *meteors*, at night. Particles from the Sun create colorful *auroras* when they strike air molecules, and dangerous ultraviolet sunlight is absorbed by the *ozone layer*. All the weather known on Earth occurs at the bottom of this vast ocean of air.

Lightning splits the sky during a severe thunderstorm in Milwaukee, Wisconsin. Lightning's spark breaks down nitrogen gas in the air, making chemicals that plants need to grow.

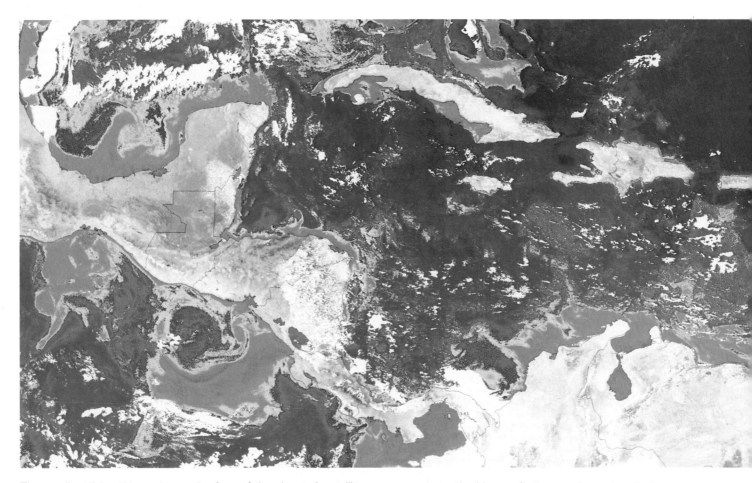

The smallest living things change the face of the planet. A satellite camera captures the bloom of microscopic marine plants in the waters off Mexico and South America. The greatest amount of plant life appears red, the lowest amount is deep blue.

A World of Life

Earth is truly the living planet. Life, in all its many forms, is the planet's most important and unique feature. According to the best counts, people share the Earth with about one million different kinds of animals—most of them insects—and more than 350,000 types of plants.

Living creatures helped make Earth the haven it now is. Most scientists believe that Earth's atmosphere started changing billions of years ago, when marine plants with the ability to make their own food first appeared. These plants contained a green pigment called *chlorophyll*—the only substance in nature able to trap and store the energy in sunlight.

Through the process of *photosynthesis*, green plants use sunlight, water, and carbon dioxide gas to make sugar. They also give off water and oxygen gas, shaping the atmosphere human beings breathe. With satellite cameras sensitive to chlorophyll, the importance of plants to human existence is seen. Colonies of tiny marine plants bloom around Earth's coastlines. Far from the continents, where rivers and ocean currents bring nutrients to the sea surface, the plants don't grow as well.

This nighttime photograph of the United States reveals a constellation of city lights. Even from space, the planet easily shows the marks of human activity.

When astronauts look down on Earth from a spaceship, they do not need special equipment to find signs of life. For example, the lush green valley of Africa's Nile River traces a dark line through the light-colored sands of the Sahara Desert.

Many signs of human activity stand out sharply. One famous landmark is the Great Wall of China, which runs 1,500 miles (2,400 kilometers) inland from the Yellow Sea. Cities of steel and concrete form dark splotches on the subtle shadings of nature. With a telescope, astronauts could look down upon canals and harbors, highways and airports.

Although space explorers can see these things from their vantage point far above Earth, they must look carefully to find them. A more obvious sign of human life awaits on the night side of Earth. As the Sun sets on the spaceship, the darkened Earth seems to fill with stars. Beneath, where millions of people fight off the darkness, the twinkling glow of city lights reveals a coastline. Only a flash of lightning from an evening thunderstorm challenges these human-made constellations.

The Moon's familiar face rises above a cloudy Earth. It is Earth's nearest neighbor in space, circling the planet once each month. The only celestial body on which humans have landed, the Moon has become a stepping stone into the solar system.

The Moon: Our Neighbor in Space

The Moon is Earth's partner in space. About 2,160 miles (3,476 kilometers) across, the Moon is an airless, waterless world just one-fourth the size of Earth. It circles the planet once every twenty-seven days at an average distance of about 238,000 miles (384,000 kilometers).

Only one side of the Moon is visible from Earth. The pull of the Earth's gravity slowed the Moon's spin until it exactly matched the twenty-seven-day orbital period. Now the Moon completes one rotation in exactly the same time it takes to circle the Earth.

As the Moon slides along in its orbit, it rises into the skies about fifty minutes later each day. The sunlit portion of the Moon's surface—the part visible from Earth—changes daily in a cycle called the Moon's *phases.* When the Moon is new, it lies in the same direction as the Sun. It cannot be seen from Earth because only its dark night side faces the planet. As the Moon moves eastward, its sunlit side grows from a slender crescent into a full, bright disk (Full Moon). Continuing on in its orbit, the Moon shrinks from disk, to crescent, and finally back to New Moon.

Marked by ancient basins and giant craters, the Moon's surface has changed very little since it formed. The most important change, at least as far as people are concerned, occurred in 1969. That was when astronauts first set foot on the dusty lunar plains.

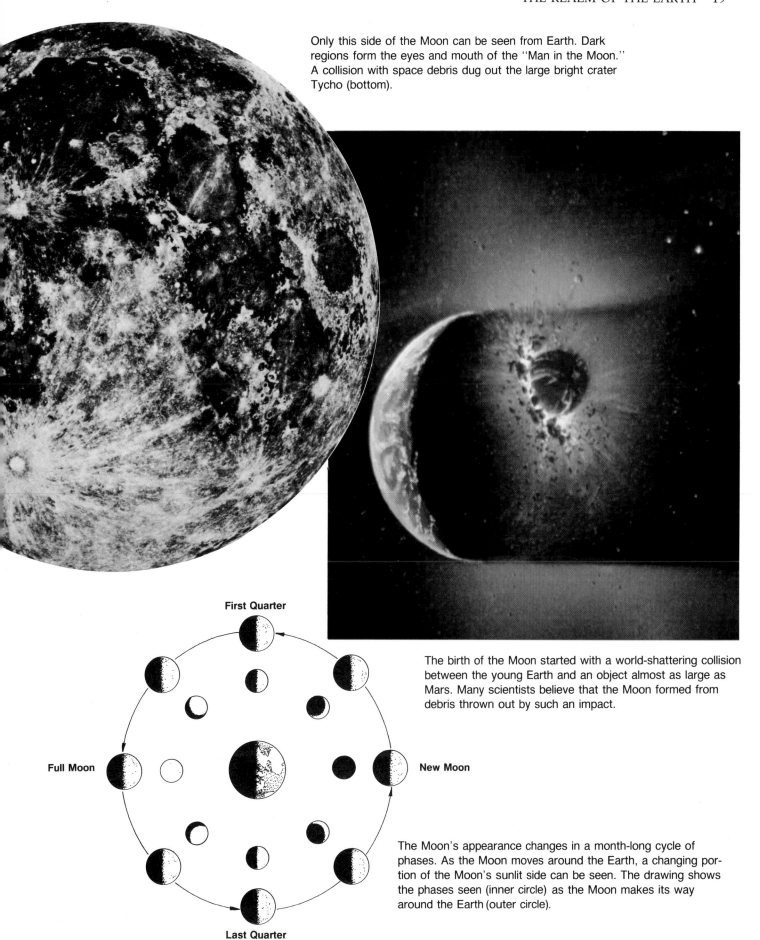

Only this side of the Moon can be seen from Earth. Dark regions form the eyes and mouth of the "Man in the Moon." A collision with space debris dug out the large bright crater Tycho (bottom).

The birth of the Moon started with a world-shattering collision between the young Earth and an object almost as large as Mars. Many scientists believe that the Moon formed from debris thrown out by such an impact.

First Quarter

Full Moon

New Moon

Last Quarter

The Moon's appearance changes in a month-long cycle of phases. As the Moon moves around the Earth, a changing portion of the Moon's sunlit side can be seen. The drawing shows the phases seen (inner circle) as the Moon makes its way around the Earth (outer circle).

Venus: A Tortured World

I f astronauts headed away from Earth, toward the Sun, they would reach Venus first. With its dense, cloud-filled atmosphere, Venus at first seems like a slightly smaller version of Earth. There the similarities end. Venus is a hot, desert world topped by an unbroken layer of acid clouds.

Venus is one of the brightest objects in Earth's sky. Only the Sun and Moon exceed Venus's brilliance, and at its brightest Venus even casts faint shadows. When its orbit swings Venus closest to Earth, it passes only twenty-five million miles (forty million kilometers) away. That is only about one hundred times farther than the Moon, which makes Venus the closest planet to Earth.

Ancient civilizations, especially the Maya people of Mexico, carefully watched the movements of Venus. Because Venus orbits closer to the Sun than Earth, the planet is alternately seen in the evening and morning skies; Venus is never seen all night long. Instead it is in view for only a few hours each night, when it rises before dawn or sets after sundown.

When Venus is highest in the evening sky, it begins a slow fall toward the horizon. After about three months, it disappears into the glare of the setting Sun and quickly moves to the other side of its orbit. Emerging into the morning sky, Venus takes three more months to reach its highest point. Another six months must pass before it again becomes visible in the evening.

Seen through a telescope, Venus shows different phases as it circles the Sun. It changes from a crescent to a disk, like the Moon. Sunlight reflects off the planet's clouds but reveals nothing of what lies beneath them.

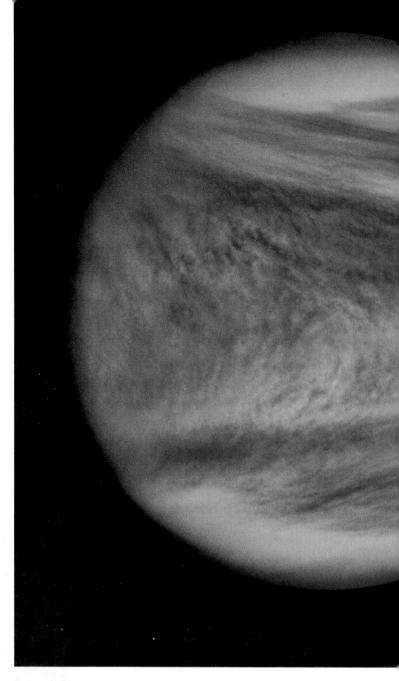

Thick, reflective clouds make Venus the third brightest object in the sky—and permanently hide its surface from easy view.

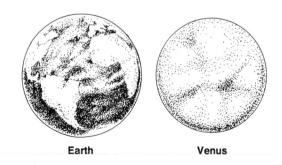

Earth **Venus**

Earth and Venus, largest of the rocky planets, were once thought to be twins. But with a hot, waterless surface and acidic clouds, Venus is an astronaut's nightmare.

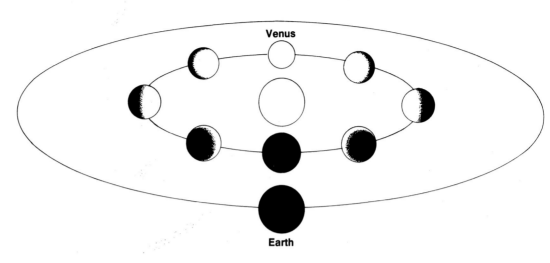

Because Venus circles closer to the Sun than Earth, it runs through a cycle of phases like those of the Moon. Venus is full when on the far side of Sun; it is new when its night side faces Earth.

Facts About Venus

Diameter:
7,521 miles (12,104 km), or 95% that of Earth

Surface Temperature:
867° F (464° C)

Surface Pressure:
90 times that of Earth's, equivalent to the pressure at a water depth of 3,000 feet (900 meters) on Earth

Atmosphere:
96% carbon dioxide

Length of Day:
243 days, 14 minutes
Planet spins opposite to rotation of Earth

Satellites:
None

Using radar to peek through the clouds, space probes have found continent-like land masses on Venus. The largest, Aphrodite (yellow and green), is half of Africa's size.

Length of Year:
224.7 days

Distance from Sun:
67,241,000 miles (108,209,000 km), or 72% that of Earth

Until scientists learned the truth about conditions on Venus, the planet was often called Earth's twin. Earth and Venus are the largest of the solar system's inner planets, are about the same size, and have thick, cloudy atmospheres. Since Venus was closer to the Sun, it would naturally be a little hotter than Earth. The popular view painted Venus as a hot, steamy, tropical planet. Nothing could be further from the truth.

The first surprise came in the 1950s, when astronomers first measured the temperature of Venus. The surface was over 850° F (450° C). This was no tropical paradise, but an inferno twice as hot as a household oven. No liquid water could exist there—even tin and lead would melt. Carbon dioxide, the major gas in the atmosphere, acts as a heat trap that keeps Venus from cooling off.

In the 1960s astronomers used radar to penetrate the cloudy veil and measure how fast Venus spins. They found that it barely spins at all, completing one orbit around the Sun (one year) in less time than it takes to make one turn on its axis (one day). A Venus day is therefore longer than its year. Astronomers also found that Venus rotates in the direction opposite to the Earth and most other planets.

From 1961 to 1990, twenty-four American and Soviet space missions have visited Venus. They have gathered a lot of information. The bright yellow clouds that blanket Venus are made from droplets of sulfuric acid. Drops may become large enough to fall like rain, but evaporate before reaching the ground. At the surface, the dense atmosphere presses down with a force ninety times greater than that of the Earth's. This pressure is equal to the pressure felt half a mile (about one kilometer) under the ocean.

In this painting, the Soviet Union's spacecraft *Venera 14* lands on Venus. It had only about two hours to send scientists its findings before the searing heat destroyed it.

Eleven spacecraft have actually touched down and transmitted information from the surface of Venus, and four Soviet landers even sent back pictures. They plunged through acid clouds and settled onto rocky plains, experiencing directly the searing heat of Venus and the crushing weight of its atmosphere. Most of these probes lasted less than two hours.

Why study such a forbidding place? In many ways, Venus is Earth's twin. How could two planets so similar in size and distance from the Sun turn out to be so different? The hostile environment of Venus holds secrets that will help us better understand how the Earth has changed.

Aphrodite, the largest "continent" on Venus, could span the United States from coast to coast. Aphrodite's eastern and western mountains hold some of the planet's roughest terrain.

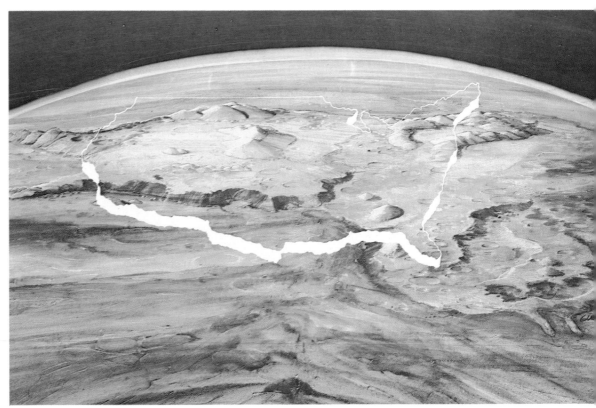

Venera 14 sent this picture from Venus in 1982. The view looks down at the craft's base (left) and out toward the distant horizon (top right). Sunlight filtered through the thick clouds bathes the scene in an eerie orange light.

Mars: The Red Planet

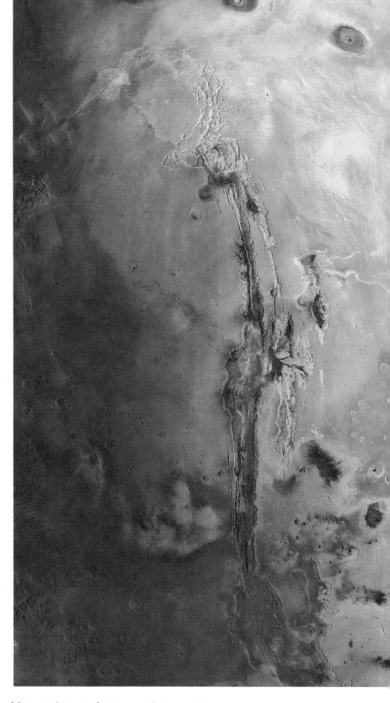

The planet Mars, the second-closest planet to Earth, has long fascinated people. Many ancient civilizations associated its reddish color with the blood of battle and named the planet for their gods of war. Mars is the name of the Roman war god.

In the nineteenth century, Mars excited astronomers as improved telescopes revealed fine detail on the planet. During periods when Mars is closest to the Earth, called *opposition*, observers reported many features, such as blurry white or yellow patches and straight, dark lines. They watched as each gleaming polar ice cap grew during the Martian winter and faded during summer. They realized that the white patches were clouds, while the bright yellow spots were billowing dust storms.

In 1895, an American astronomer named Percival Lowell presented dramatic ideas of life on Mars. He imagined intelligent beings struggling for survival on a dying world. The feeble gravity of Mars cannot keep water in the atmosphere from escaping into space. The strange lines were giant canals, constructed to transport water from the ice caps to the dying cities. H. G. Wells based his 1898 tale of a Martian invasion, called *The War of the Worlds*, on these ideas.

But Lowell's ideas have proved incorrect. The straight lines were merely illusions. Martian air is far too thin and dry for any beings. Spacecraft have looked, but have failed to find, any life on Mars.

Mars makes up for its small size with a vast canyon complex (center) and volcanoes that dwarf any on Earth. A morning mist fills the western canyons, and two small volcanoes rise out of a thin veil of cloud (top).

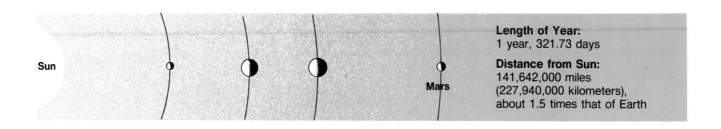

Sun

Mars

Length of Year:
1 year, 321.73 days

Distance from Sun:
141,642,000 miles
(227,940,000 kilometers),
about 1.5 times that of Earth

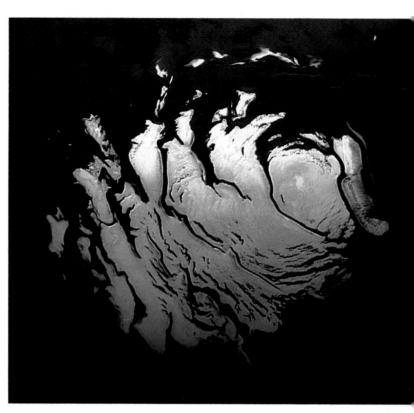

Ice caps the north and south poles of Mars. This picture shows the shrunken south cap during a Martian summer. Unlike the north cap, it contains frozen carbon dioxide, or dry ice, not water.

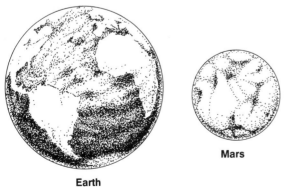

Earth

Mars

Mars has an atmosphere too thin to breathe, a cold climate, and no liquid water on the surface. Still, it is the most comfortable planet for future human exploration.

Facts About Mars

Diameter:
4,222 miles (6,794 km), or 53% that of Earth

Average Surface Temperature:
−13° F (−25° C)

Surface Pressure:
0.7% (1/150th) that of Earth

Atmosphere:
95% carbon dioxide, 2.7% nitrogen

Length of Day:
24 hours, 37 minutes

Satellites:
2

Satellite Data

Name	Size	Discovered
Phobos	17 x 12 miles (28 x 20 km)	1877
Deimos	10 x 7 miles (16 x 12 km)	1877

In this painting, thin clouds ring the solar system's largest known volcano—Olympus Mons. It towers fifteen miles (twenty-four kilometers) above the Martian lava plains it helped create.

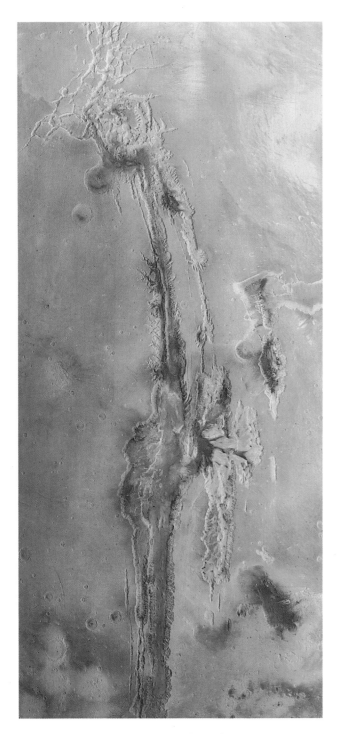

This great valley, named Valles Marineris, cuts across one-fourth of Mars. About 3,100 miles (5,000 kilometers) long, it is four miles (seven kilometers) deep in places.

Although the idea of a Martian civilization has long disappeared, the planet Mars continues to fascinate scientists. It is, after all, the planet most like Earth. About half of Earth's size, Mars takes 24.6 hours to spin on its axis, about forty minutes longer than a day on Earth. Mars has enormous volcanoes, vast canyons, dune fields, and dry channels carved by liquid water.

The planet's most remarkable feature is Valles Marineris, a canyon complex that runs 3,100 miles (5,000 kilometers) across the planet. It dwarfs any similar feature on Earth. It is so long that one end can be in full sunlight while the other is immersed in the cold Martian night. The temperature difference sends winds raging along the valley.

Despite their similarities, Mars and Earth are still quite different. On a typical Martian summer day, the temperature rises no higher than the freezing point, or 32° F (0° C.) After sundown, heat escapes quickly through the thin air and most areas cool to about −148° F (−100° C). The atmosphere has no protective ozone layer, so deadly ultraviolet light from the Sun reaches the surface. The atmosphere exerts so little pressure that any liquid water spilled on the surface would evaporate in

In 1976, cameras on the U.S. *Viking 1* lander first transmitted pictures of the rock-strewn surface of Mars. Small sand dunes stretch toward the horizon. Windblown dust thrown high in the atmosphere colors the sky pink.

Mars has two small, potato-shaped moons. Phobos (top) shows many craters and strange groove-like markings, although Deimos (bottom) looks less rugged. Named for the mythical sons of Mars, Fear and Terror, the moons once may have been Sun-circling asteroids.

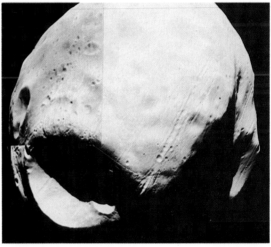

seconds. Channels show that water once ran on Mars, but they probably formed when volcanoes melted ice below the surface. Mars is now drier than any desert on Earth.

In 1976, two American *Viking* landers set down on the surface of Mars while companion spacecraft viewed the planet from orbit. The landers searched the soil for microbes— germ-sized life—without success. They returned images of boulder-strewn fields, sand dunes, and a weird pink sky. Scientists are planning more missions to Mars to further examine the Red Planet.

Mercury: The Sun-Skimmer

Mercury, closer to the Sun than Venus, is named for the swift-footed messenger of the Roman gods. It is the right name for this tiny world. Mercury orbits closer to the Sun than any other planet, circling it once every eighty-eight days. From Earth, Mercury is never seen high in the sky or far from the glow of twilight. In fact, it is hard to see Mercury at all.

Astronomers once thought that Mercury took as long to spin on its axis as it did to orbit the Sun. In other words, it seemed that Mercury's day was as long as the eighty-eight-day Mercury-year. By bouncing radar beams off Mercury in 1965, astronomers learned that the planet actually rotates once every 58.6 days.

Mercury has the most lopsided orbit of any planet except Pluto. It swoops to within twenty-nine million miles (forty-seven million kilometers) of the Sun's surface. At closest approach, the daytime temperature may reach 840° F (450° C). Mercury then pulls out to a distance of forty-four million miles (seventy million kilometers). Closest to the Sun, when the planet is moving fastest, its orbital speed outpaces its speed of rotation. As a result, astronauts at some locations on the planet could see *two* sunrises and sunsets each Mercury day.

Like Venus, Mercury shows phases when viewed through a telescope—but little else. Aside from a few vague markings, the landscape of Mercury was a mystery until spacecraft visited the planet. In 1974 and 1975, an American probe named *Mariner 10* made three close approaches to Mercury. It photographed half the planet's surface, and discovered a feeble atmosphere made from gas particles captured from the Sun.

The pictures show that Mercury looks much like the Earth's Moon, a heavily cratered surface with occasional plains made during ancient lava floods. Except for new craters carved by occasional meteorites, Mercury's battered landscape has remained unchanged for eons.

Sun	Mercury	Length of Year:	Distance from Sun:
		87.97 days	35,985,000 miles (57,909,000 kilometers), or 39% that of Earth

Earth   Mercury

Mercury is about one-third Earth's size.

Facts About Mercury

Diameter:
3,031 miles (4,878 km), or 38% that
of Earth

Average Surface Temperature:
340° F, (171° C)

Atmosphere:
Extremely thin, contains helium and
hydrogen

Length of Day:
58 days, 15 hours, 30 minutes

Satellites:
None

Mercury orbits closest to the Sun. Its
rugged landscape is baked to 370° F
(188° C) by day, frozen to −290° F
(−180° C) by night.

High mountains ring Mercury's
Caloris Basin. About 800 miles
(roughly 1,300 kilometers) across, it
formed when a small asteroid struck
Mercury.

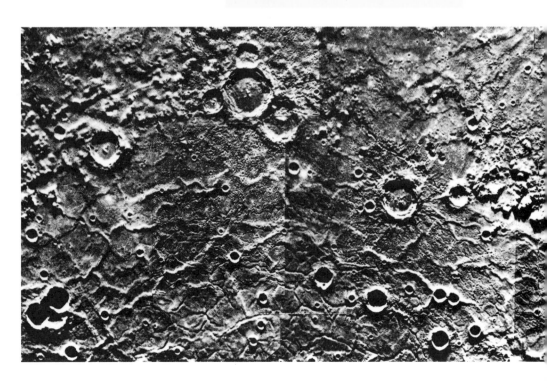

Asteroids and Meteors: Cosmic Debris

On New Year's Day, 1801, an Italian monk and astronomer named Giuseppe Piazzi discovered an unusual object. After weeks of observation, it was clear that the object circled the Sun between Mars and Jupiter. Piazzi named his find Ceres.

By 1808 astronomers had found three more bodies moving in similar paths. They were named Pallas, Juno, and Vesta. All four bodies were only a few hundred miles across—far too small to be considered planets. Instead, they turned out to be the largest members of a group of objects astronomers call *asteroids*.

Today, astronomers know of some 2,200 asteroids. Most orbit the Sun at distances between 2.2 and 3.2 times farther than Earth, placing them in the gap between Mars and Jupiter. This has come to be called the asteroid belt.

Why study asteroids? First, collisions between asteroids break off fragments that may find their way to Earth's surface as *meteorites.* Second, asteroids represent material that never quite formed into a planet. Finally, asteroids have repeatedly collided with the planets, and may have changed the course of life on Earth.

Startled pterosaurs take to the air as a fragmenting asteroid slams into Earth. Beneath the rising fireball (center), a giant crater has formed and the body of one fragment has been destroyed. A scene like this sixty-five million years ago may have started the demise of the dinosaurs.

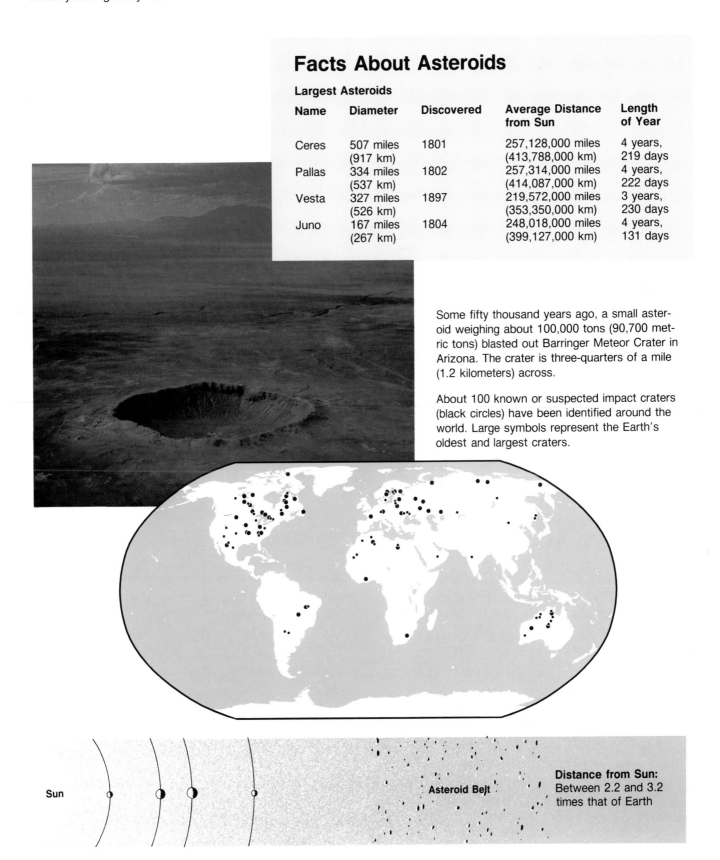

Facts About Asteroids

Largest Asteroids

Name	Diameter	Discovered	Average Distance from Sun	Length of Year
Ceres	507 miles (917 km)	1801	257,128,000 miles (413,788,000 km)	4 years, 219 days
Pallas	334 miles (537 km)	1802	257,314,000 miles (414,087,000 km)	4 years, 222 days
Vesta	327 miles (526 km)	1897	219,572,000 miles (353,350,000 km)	3 years, 230 days
Juno	167 miles (267 km)	1804	248,018,000 miles (399,127,000 km)	4 years, 131 days

Some fifty thousand years ago, a small asteroid weighing about 100,000 tons (90,700 metric tons) blasted out Barringer Meteor Crater in Arizona. The crater is three-quarters of a mile (1.2 kilometers) across.

About 100 known or suspected impact craters (black circles) have been identified around the world. Large symbols represent the Earth's oldest and largest craters.

Sun

Asteroid Belt

Distance from Sun: Between 2.2 and 3.2 times that of Earth

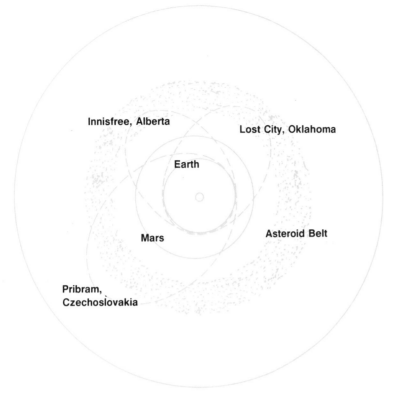

The orbits of three recovered meteorites show that the objects spent much of their time within the asteroid belt. The place-names tell where each of the meteorites landed on Earth.

The 59-ton (53.5-metric-ton) *Ahnighito*—or *tent*—meteorite, the second largest ever found, was brought from Greenland to New York City in 1897. Residents of Greenland had used its metal to make knives and spears.

Meteorites are space rocks that survive the fiery passage through the Earth's atmosphere. They are usually classified as irons, stony-irons, or stones depending on the amount of metal they contain. Only about 2,500 meteorites are known. The largest is the 66-ton (59.9-metric-ton) Hoba iron, which lies where it fell in Namibia, a country in Africa. The second largest, a 59-ton (53.5-metric-ton) meteorite recovered from Greenland, is on display at the Hayden Planetarium in New York City.

In space these objects are called *meteoroids.* They strike the Earth's atmosphere at speeds up to twenty-five miles (forty kilometers) per second. At a height of about 80 miles (128 kilometers), friction with the atmosphere surrounds the object with hot, glowing air. This fireball streaks toward Earth, becoming visible as a bright *meteor.* If it does not break up, the meteoroid will strike the surface and become a meteorite.

Meteors from much smaller particles, about as large as grains of sand, can be seen almost any dark night. The best chance of seeing meteors occurs during *meteor showers,* when Earth passes through streams of dust left behind by comets. Meteor showers do not, however, produce a greater number of meteorites than other times.

When first discovered, asteroids were thought to be the remains of a planet that had somehow broken apart. Yet the combined mass of all the asteroids amounts to only about 1/30th the mass of Earth's Moon. Asteroids and the meteoroids they create are interplanetary rubble, debris left over from the formation of the planets.

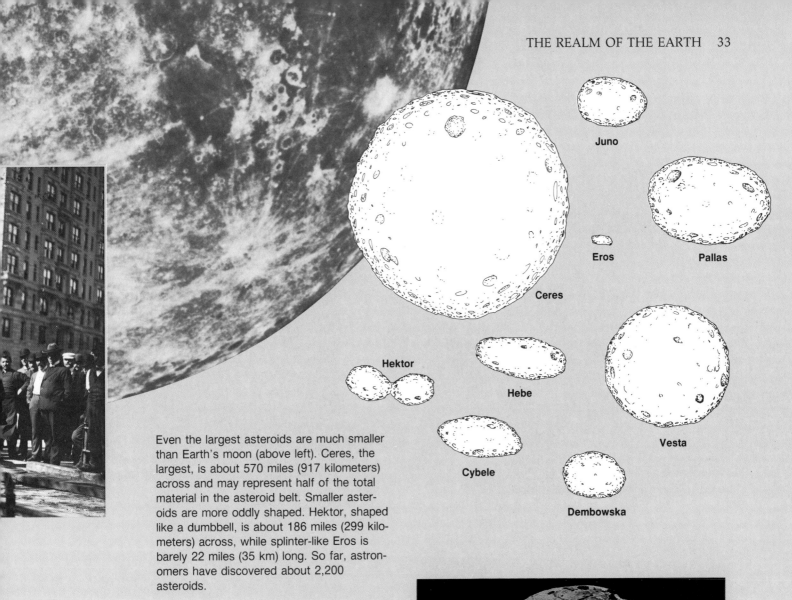

Even the largest asteroids are much smaller than Earth's moon (above left). Ceres, the largest, is about 570 miles (917 kilometers) across and may represent half of the total material in the asteroid belt. Smaller asteroids are more oddly shaped. Hektor, shaped like a dumbbell, is about 186 miles (299 kilometers) across, while splinter-like Eros is barely 22 miles (35 km) long. So far, astronomers have discovered about 2,200 asteroids.

Not all asteroids stay within the asteroid belt. One family of asteroids known as *Apollo objects* follow paths that carry them across the orbit of Earth. In 1989, one such object passed within 500,000 miles (800,000 kilometers) of Earth, or only about twice the distance to the Moon.

Most scientists now believe that an asteroid impact sixty-five million years ago led to the extinction of many plants and animals, including the dinosaurs. Asteroids may also explain several other extinctions. So while there is now no immediate threat of a collision with an asteroid, Earth has been hit in the past . . . and will be hit again.

Ceres, the first asteroid discovered, is almost twice the size of any other. It could be considered a tiny planet.

Cold and Dark Worlds

An ice geyser sends a plume of nitrogen ice miles above the surface of Neptune's moon, Triton. The planets in the outer solar system are very different from the small rocky worlds that circle close to the Sun. These giant planets are huge balls of gas many times larger than Earth.

Jupiter: King of the Planets

Jupiter serves as a colorful backdrop for two of its large moons, Io and Europa. They are both about the same size as Earth's Moon. Io appears in front of the Great Red Spot (left), a long-lived oval storm in Jupiter's atmosphere.

Jupiter, the fifth planet out from the Sun, is by far the solar system's largest world. To span Jupiter's equator would take eleven Earths. If all the other bodies in the solar system could be squeezed together, they would still account for less than half of Jupiter's mass. In other words, the solar system consists of the Sun, Jupiter, and debris.

Sometimes Jupiter is called a "star that failed." Most astronomers agree that a star needs about eighty times Jupiter's mass to turn on its nuclear fires. Jupiter does, however, give off more heat than it receives from the Sun. This internal heat is the energy left over from Jupiter's formation over 4.5 billion years ago.

Jupiter is made of the same material as stars, mostly hydrogen and helium. Like the other giant planets, Jupiter has no solid surface. About 620 miles (1,000 kilometers) beneath Jupiter's cloud tops, the enormous pressure turns hydrogen gas into a vast sea of liquid hydrogen. Jupiter spins so fast—once every ten hours—that its liquid mass bulges far outward at the equator.

Storms rage in Jupiter's colorful atmosphere. Lightning is ten thousand times as powerful as what is seen on Earth. All in all, Jupiter is rightly named for the lord of the Roman gods.

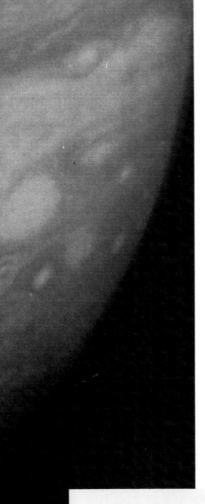

Even Jupiter's weather systems dwarf those of Earth. Here the blue-white disk of Earth is scaled to Jupiter's Great Red Spot, a storm system first seen more than 300 years ago.

Facts About Jupiter

Diameter:	Temperature at Cloud Tops:	Atmosphere:	Length of Day:	Satellites:
88,700 miles (142,800 km), or 11.3 times Earth's	−234° F (−148° C)	90% hydrogen, 10% helium	9 hours, 56 minutes	16

Largest Satellites

Name	Diameter	Discovered
Europa	1,950 miles (3,138 km)	1610
Io	2,255 miles (3,630 km)	1610
Callisto	2,982 miles (4,800 km)	1610
Ganymede	3,269 miles (5,262 km)	1610

Earth

Jupiter

By any measure, Jupiter is the solar system's giant. To equal Jupiter's bulk would take 318 Earths. Over 1,300 Earth-sized balls could fit within this enormous planet.

Sun

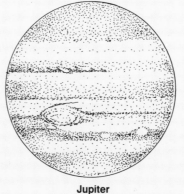

Length of Year:
11 years, 314.96 days

Distance from Sun:
483,631,000 miles
(778,292,000 km),
or 5.2 times Earth's

Jupiter

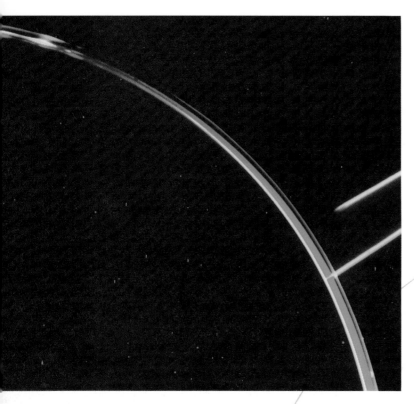

The discovery by *Voyager 1* of a thin ring around Jupiter was a surprise to scientists. Made of tiny dust particles, the ring is much too faint to see from Earth.

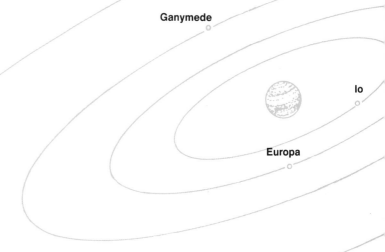

In many ways, Jupiter and its sixteen moons resemble a miniature solar system. The cartoon below shows Jupiter and the orbits of its four largest moons. The drawing is not to scale.

Callisto

Ganymede

Io

Europa

The first person to examine Jupiter in detail was the Italian scientist Galileo Galilei. In 1610, he became the first to study the planets with a telescope and discovered the four largest moons of Jupiter.

The largest of the four moons, Ganymede, is the largest satellite in the solar system. It is even bigger than the planet Mercury. Ganymede is a cratered ice ball mostly made of frozen water. Photographs taken from the *Voyager* spacecraft suggest that the ice may be broken into plates like Earth's rocky crust.

Callisto, another moon of Jupiter, orbits nearly twice as far from Jupiter as Ganymede. A huge feature called the Valhalla Basin is this moon's biggest attraction. Long ago, a large meteoroid slammed into Callisto. The heat instantly melted part of the moon's icy crust, forming a small sea that quickly refroze. Fractured rings of ice extend twelve hundred miles (two thousand kilometers) from the basin's center.

Europa, the smallest of Jupiter's big moons, is a bit smaller than Earth's Moon and remarkably smooth. The difference between its highest and lowest elevations may be as little as 330 feet (100 meters). Beneath a three-mile (five kilometer) thick crust of ice, Europa may have a deep ocean of water.

Jupiter's moon Io is probably the weirdest place in the solar system. Scientists were surprised to find nine active volcanoes during the *Voyager* flyby. The activity all over Io is greater than the most active volcanic hot spots on Earth. Umbrella-shaped plumes of sulfur compounds blast over 100 miles (160 kilometers) into Io's airless sky. The compounds give Io its unique colors.

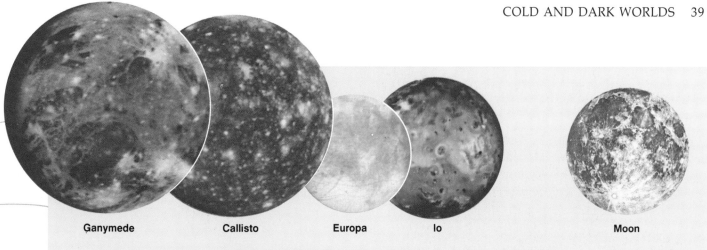

Ganymede   **Callisto**   **Europa**   **Io**   **Moon**

Of Jupiter's four largest satellites, only Europa is smaller than Earth's Moon. Ganymede is actually a bit larger than the planet Mercury.

A new volcano blasts a plume of sulfur compounds high above Io's bizarre landscape. Nearby, a black puddle of molten sulfur still oozes from an older vent.

Saturn: The Ring Maker

Saturn may be the most beautiful planet in the solar system. Although its splendid rings are no longer considered unique—all the giant planets have them—they are easily the brightest and most complex.

Saturn is second in size only to Jupiter. Like Jupiter and the other giants, Saturn is mostly made of hydrogen and helium. Under the crushing weight of its atmosphere, hydrogen gas is squeezed into a liquid ocean some 620 miles (1,000 kilometers) beneath the clouds.

Saturn is more loosely packed than Jupiter. Saturn's spin, only slightly slower than Jupiter's, gives it the greatest equatorial bulge of any planet. Saturn's loose packing lets it bulge more easily than the other planets. In fact, Saturn is not even as dense as water. If the solar system were a vast ocean, Saturn would float on the surface like a giant buoy.

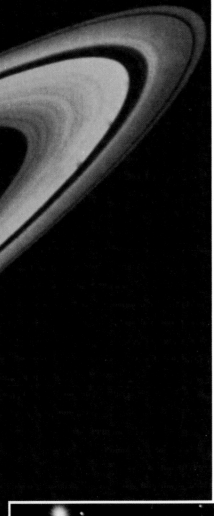

A complex system of bright, icy rings gives Saturn its unique appearance. The moons Tethys and Dione appear beneath the planet.

Facts About Saturn

Diameter:
75,000 miles (120,700 km), or 9.4 times that of Earth

Temperature at Cloud Tops:
−288° F (−178° C)

Atmosphere:
94% hydrogen, 5% helium

Length of Day:
10 hours, 41 minutes

Satellites:
17

Largest Satellites

Name	Diameter	Discovered
Titan	3,200 miles (5,150 km)	1655
Rhea	951 miles (1,530 km)	1672
Iapetus	907 miles (1,460 km)	1671
Dione	696 miles (1,120 km)	1684
Tethys	659 miles (1,060 km)	1684

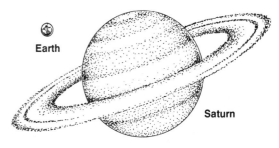

Earth

Saturn

Although Saturn is nearly ten times Earth's size, it contains more liquids and icy substances than rock. Placed in a large enough ocean, Saturn could float.

Scientists used information from *Voyager 2* to create this computer painting of the craft's 1981 flyby of Saturn.

Length of Year:
29 years, 167.25 days

Distance from Sun:
888,210,000 miles (1,429,370,000 km), or 9.6 times that of Earth

Saturn

Cloud bands in Saturn's atmosphere seem less distinct and show fewer colors than those at Jupiter. Several factors help to blur Saturn's clouds. The planet's greater distance from the Sun (nearly twice that of Jupiter) means much colder temperatures. That means clouds start forming at much lower levels. The weaker gravity of Saturn does not pull the atmosphere together as strongly as Jupiter. This makes for thicker clouds. Therefore, Saturn makes its clouds thicker and at lower altitudes than Jupiter, which makes details harder to see.

Saturn's hallmark is its magnificent ring system. The rings were first observed by the Dutch scientist Christian Huygens in 1656. Tip to tip, Saturn's rings measure about 170,300 (274,000 kilometers) across or about 70 percent of the distance between Earth and Moon. Yet the rings are quite thin, perhaps less than fifty feet (fifteen meters) with occasional waves rising and falling by up to a mile (1.6 kilometers). The surface area of Saturn's ring system is about eighty times greater than the total surface area of the Earth.

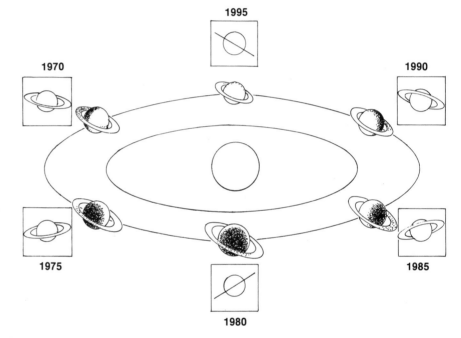

As Saturn moves along in its thirty-year orbit at a 27° tilt, the rings can be seen from different angles. In the diagram at right, boxes show how Saturn would look through a telescope in different parts of its orbit. Every fifteen years, the rings appear to be on edge and almost disappear. This will next happen in 1995.

The large, icy moons of Saturn are all smaller than Earth's Moon. Tethys, Dione, and Rhea are heavily cratered iceballs. One hemisphere of strange Iapetus is coated with a very dark substance.

The rings are not solid, but made up of billions of small ice particles. The smallest are the size of sugar grains; the largest are as big as houses. There are six main regions in the ring system. Detailed photographs from spacecraft revealed thousands upon thousands of mini-rings within each one. The rings may be debris that never formed into a moon, or the remains of a moon that broke up.

Saturn has at least seventeen moons and probably many more. Titan, its largest, is the only moon with a thick atmosphere—thicker even than that of Earth. Titan is slightly smaller than Jupiter's Ganymede, but a bit larger than the planet Mercury. Its atmosphere is about 125 miles (200 kilometers) thick and mainly consists of nitrogen. Sunlight acting on a small amount of methane in Titan's atmosphere produces an orange smog of haze particles.

The haze completely hides Titan's −288° F (−178° C) surface from view. The haze particles may stick together and grow, eventually falling to Titan's surface as a strange drizzle.

Since the frigid surface is cold enough for methane gas to turn liquid, methane seas may exist on Titan.

Another of Saturn's strange moons is Iapetus. One side is a bright, cratered, icy surface, but the other side is only one-fifth as bright. Some scientists think that the moon sweeps up dark material as it orbits Saturn, but others suggest it may have oozed up from within Iapetus. No one is certain why Iapetus exhibits this two-faced appearance.

Titan's cloud-filled atmosphere, the thickest of any moon, completely hides its surface. Titan is larger than the planet Mercury and only slightly smaller than Jupiter's big moon Ganymede.

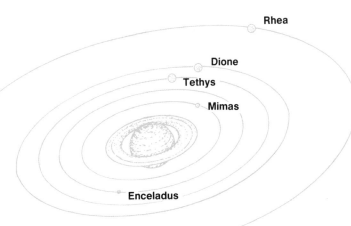

This cartoon shows the relationship between Saturn and the orbits of its largest moons. The moons are not drawn to scale.

Uranus: A World on Its Side

Until 1781, Saturn was the farthest planet known to astronomers. That changed on March 13, when English astronomer William Herschel noticed a fuzzy, blue-green patch of light while scanning the sky with his telescope. Herschel at first thought he had found a comet. But calculations of the object's orbit showed that it was in fact a planet, the first to be found in recorded history. Herschel called it *Georgium Sidem*, or George's Star, in honor of England's King George III. But others suggested the name of the Roman god of the sky—Uranus.

Since Uranus lies about twice as far from the Sun as Saturn, its discovery instantly doubled the size of the solar system astronomers knew. The planet is about four times the size of Earth, making it the third largest gas giant. It takes about eighty-four years to complete one orbit around the Sun. Like Jupiter and Saturn, Uranus is mostly made of hydrogen and helium. Its atmosphere also contains a small amount of methane. Methane absorbs the red light in sunlight and reflects the rest, giving Uranus its blue-green color.

Uranus takes almost seventeen hours to spin on its axis. But the axis itself is tipped over 98° to the plane of its orbit. Unlike the other planets, which spin like tops as they circle the Sun, Uranus seems to be rolling along its orbit. Perhaps long ago an object larger than Earth smashed into Uranus, tipping the planet on its side. The planet's tilt exposes it to the Sun in a strange way. Uranus faces one pole, then the other into the Sun. Each pole receives forty-two years of uninterrupted sunlight, followed by an equal period of total darkness. These are the seasons of Uranus.

It would be difficult to imagine a disk more bland than that of Uranus. Only a few thin, featureless clouds were seen by *Voyager 2* in 1986. Methane gas, which absorbs the reddish colors in sunlight, gives Uranus its blue-green color.

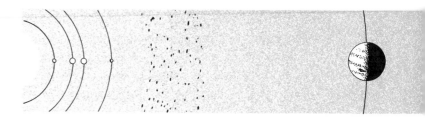

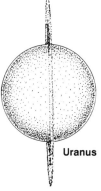

Earth

Uranus

Of the giant planets, only Uranus lacks a strong internal heat source. The distant Sun drives its weather, a fact which may explain the planet's bland appearance.

The rings of Uranus were discovered in 1977 when astronomers saw them cut off the light of a star. The particles within the eleven main rings are as black as coal.

Facts About Uranus

Discovered:
1781, by William Herschel

Diameter:
31,700 miles (51,100 km), or four times that of Earth

Temperature at Cloud Tops:
−351° F (−213° C)

Atmosphere:
85% hydrogen, 15% helium

Length of Day:
16 hours, 48 minutes. Planet spins opposite to rotation of Earth.

Satellites:
15

Largest Satellites

Name	Diameter	Discovered
Titania	982 miles (1,580 km)	1787
Oberon	947 miles (1,524 km)	1787
Umbriel	728 miles (1,172 km)	1851
Ariel	720 miles (1,158 km)	1851
Miranda	298 miles (480 km)	1948

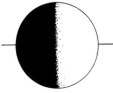

Uranus

Earth

Earth's seasons are caused by the 23.4° tilt of its axis. The north and south poles each spend about six months tilted into the Sun. But the axis of Uranus is tilted 98°. The planet's south pole gets forty-two years of full sunlight; the north pole waits that long for the next dawn.

Length of Year:
84 years, 3.65 days

Distance from Sun:
1,786,521,000 miles (2,874,993,000 km) or 19.2 times that of Earth

Uranus

Unlike Jupiter and Saturn, no brightly colored clouds swirl across the face of Uranus. The planet looks like a featureless, blue ball. Uranus is cold—about –350° F (–213° C)—and its methane clouds form very deep in the atmosphere. A smoggy haze produced by the action of sunlight on gases in the atmosphere helps smear details in the clouds below. *Voyager 2*, which in 1986 became the only spacecraft to visit Uranus, spotted only a few white methane-ice clouds.

Although no sunlight strikes one side of Uranus for decades, it is no colder than the sunlit part of the planet. Winds deep within the atmosphere must circulate heat to the dark side.

Until 1977, Saturn was the only planet known to have rings. On March 10, astronomers were watching a bright star as Uranus slowly passed in front of it. They expected the star to fade out as Uranus moved toward it. But the star dimmed and brightened several times before Uranus finally blocked its light. The star went through the same pattern after reappearing on the other side of the planet. This is how the rings of Uranus announced their presence.

The ring system, measured from tip to tip, is about 63,400 miles (102,000 kilometers) across. It contains ten major rings and a broad, smeared-out band of smaller particles. The rings are much thinner, coarser, and darker than the brilliant rings of Saturn. The brightest and farthest ring is about fifty-five miles (ninety kilometers) across at its widest point. It is only three hundred feet (ninety meters) thick. Within it are charcoal-black particles as small as a marble and as large as a melon.

Uranus has a family of fifteen satellites, ten of which were discovered by *Voyager 2*. The moons are mostly made of frozen water and other ices, but their surfaces are surprisingly dark. All four of the largest moons show evidence of ancient volcanic processes that have erased many of their oldest features. Frozen puddles of some mysterious liquid fill some of Oberon's craters. Cracks and grooves scar the faces of Titania and Ariel.

Miranda, smallest of the five major moons, is the most puzzling. Just 300 miles (480 kilometers) wide, the little moon contains landforms usually seen only on much larger worlds. When part of Miranda's icy surface slipped inward, it created huge cliffs over nine miles (fifteen kilometers) high. Collisions probably blew Miranda apart several times. When the moon reassembled, it froze into the bizarre terrain *Voyager 2* revealed.

Moon

Here, the largest moons of Uranus are compared with Earth's Moon. Dark fluid pooled in the fresh craters on Oberon, and ice once flowed along Ariel's valleys.

Miranda

Umbriel

Ariel

Oberon

Titania

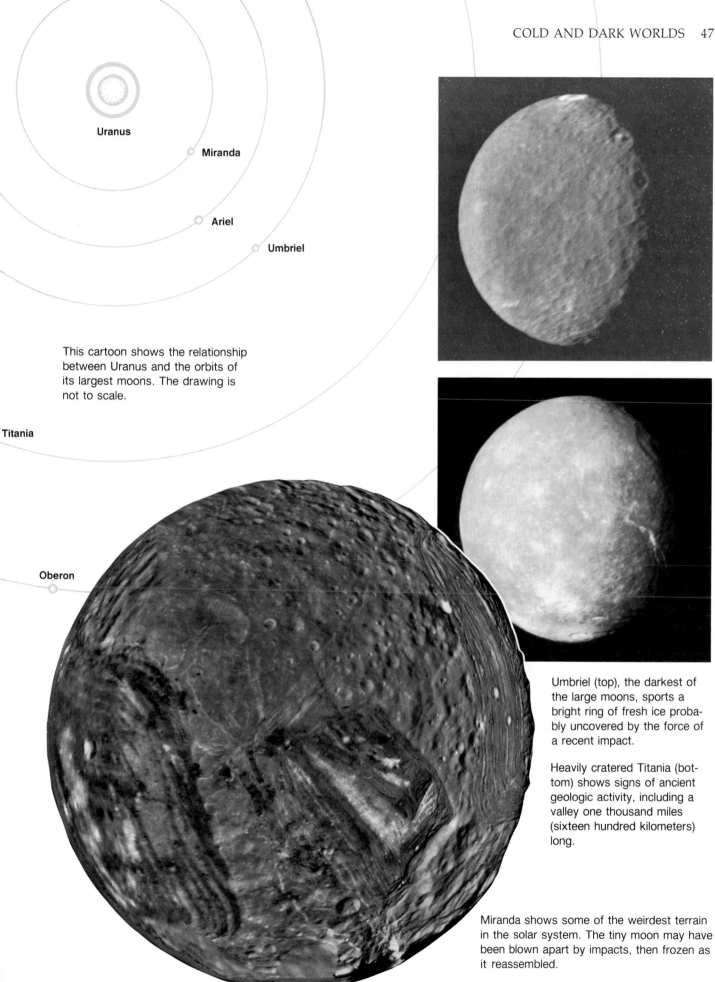

Uranus

Miranda

Ariel

Umbriel

This cartoon shows the relationship between Uranus and the orbits of its largest moons. The drawing is not to scale.

Titania

Oberon

Umbriel (top), the darkest of the large moons, sports a bright ring of fresh ice probably uncovered by the force of a recent impact.

Heavily cratered Titania (bottom) shows signs of ancient geologic activity, including a valley one thousand miles (sixteen hundred kilometers) long.

Miranda shows some of the weirdest terrain in the solar system. The tiny moon may have been blown apart by impacts, then frozen as it reassembled.

Neptune: The Last Giant

A fter the discovery of Uranus in 1781, astronomers rushed to observe the new planet so that they could examine its orbit and predict its future positions. By the early 1800s, astronomers knew something was wrong. Their calculations took into account the way the gravity of the Sun and all of the known planets pulled on Uranus, but the computed position differed from the planet's actual position in the sky.

Astronomers suggested that another new planet may be responsible for the odd behavior of Uranus. Two mathematicians, John Couch Adams in England and Urbain Le Verrier in France, computed the new planet's size and location. Neither man could convince astronomers to look for the new planet. Finally, in 1846, Le Verrier sent his results to a young German astronomer named Johann Galle. He easily spotted Neptune that evening.

Neptune, farthest of the gas giants, lies 2.8 billion miles (4.5 billion kilometers) from the Sun and takes 165 years to complete an orbit. It is slightly smaller than Uranus, but still about four times the size of Earth. Like Uranus, Neptune's bluish color comes from a small amount of methane in the deep hydrogen-helium atmosphere.

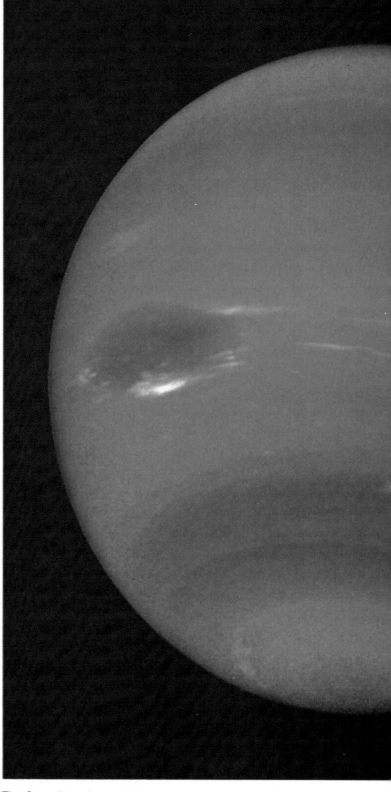

The Great Dark Spot of Neptune is a storm system similar to Jupiter's Great Red Spot. If Jupiter were cut down to Neptune's size, the spots would just about match.

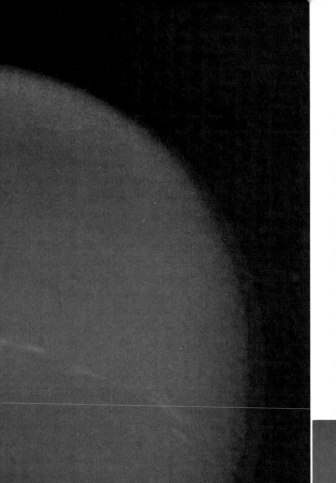

Facts About Neptune

Discovered:
1846, by Johann Galle and
Heinrich d'Arrest

Diameter:
30,200 miles (48,600 km)
or 3.8 times that of Earth

Temperature at Cloud Tops:
−357° F (−216° C)

Atmosphere:
85% hydrogen, 15% helium

Length of Day:
16 hours, 3 minutes

Satellites:
8

Largest Satellites

Name	Diameter	Discovered
Triton	1,690 miles (2,720 km)	1846
1989N1	249 miles (400 km)	1989
Neried	211 miles (340 km)	1949

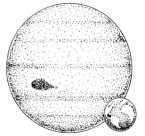

Neptune   Earth

About one-quarter Neptune's size, Earth could fit snugly within the planet's Great Dark Spot.

Crystals of frozen methane gas create bands of wispy white clouds high in Neptune's atmosphere. They cast shadows on the thick deck of blue clouds thirty miles (fifty kilometers) below.

Length of Year:
164 years, 288.54 days

Distance from Sun:
2,798,989,000 miles
(4,504,328,000 km)
or 30.1 times that of Earth

Neptune

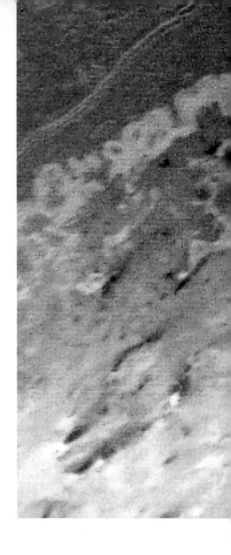

Voyager 2: Explorer of the Solar System

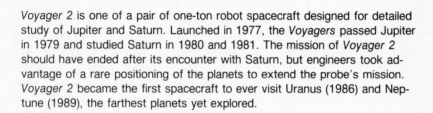

Voyager 2 is one of a pair of one-ton robot spacecraft designed for detailed study of Jupiter and Saturn. Launched in 1977, the *Voyagers* passed Jupiter in 1979 and studied Saturn in 1980 and 1981. The mission of *Voyager 2* should have ended after its encounter with Saturn, but engineers took advantage of a rare positioning of the planets to extend the probe's mission. *Voyager 2* became the first spacecraft to ever visit Uranus (1986) and Neptune (1989), the farthest planets yet explored.

During the twelve-year mission, the spacecraft returned thousands of pictures and enough data to fill six thousand sets of encyclopedias. Now racing out of the solar system, the probes begin a new life as the *Voyager* Interstellar Mission. They may send back information well into the next century.

Each *Voyager* carries a gold-plated record of music, sounds, and images of Earth. This gift from Earth will not be discovered anytime soon. Coasting at thirty-five thousand miles per hour (fifteen kilometers per second) over the next twenty thousand years, the *Voyagers* will have traveled less than one-third the distance to the nearest star.

Despite their similarities, Neptune's appearance is surprisingly unlike Uranus. The planet's most obvious feature is an enormous oval storm system dubbed the Great Dark Spot. As large as Earth, this storm dominates Neptune's blue disk. It is similar to the Great Red Spot swirling in Jupiter's clouds. A second, smaller dark spot whirls near Neptune's south polar region. Plumes of methane cirrus clouds form a thin, silvery band across the blue planet.

Like the other giant planets, Neptune has rings. The ring system measures 78,300 miles (126,000 kilometers) across and is made up of three thin rings and a broad sheet of dust particles. The outermost ring consists of several dense, relatively bright clumps of particles seemingly riding along a thin, faint ring. Scientists cannot fully explain how these clumps form.

Triton and Nereid are the only two of Neptune's eight known moons discovered from Earth. The others were found by *Voyager 2*. One of them, temporarily named 1989N1, is a dark, cratered iceball 250 miles (400 kilometers) wide—slightly larger than Nereid.

Triton, the largest moon, is 1,690 miles (2,720 kilometers) across. Since it orbits opposite to the direction of Neptune's spin, Triton may have been captured into orbit by Neptune's gravity. It now circles so close to the planet that, one day millions of years from now, Triton will be ripped asunder by Neptune's gravity and create a magnificent set of rings.

Triton is wrapped within a nitrogen atmosphere 100,000 times thinner than Earth's. It is the coldest world space probes have visited. On the moon's −400° F (−236° C) surface, nitrogen and methane gases freeze out and

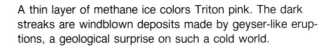

A thin layer of methane ice colors Triton pink. The dark streaks are windblown deposits made by geyser-like eruptions, a geological surprise on such a cold world.

Shown here is the bright southern hemisphere of Neptune's largest moon, Triton. Nitrogen and methane frost coats the moon. With a surface temperature of −400° F (−236° C), Triton is the coldest object space probes have ever visited.

coat Triton with gleaming frost. Few craters show up on Triton, which means that icy flows have resurfaced the moon in the recent past.

Triton's most surprising features are its ice geysers. Dark surface streaks up to forty-seven miles (seventy-five kilometers) long represent material shot high into the atmosphere and blown about by winds. Close examination of *Voyager 2* images revealed at least two eruptions in progress. They may be powered by pools of liquid nitrogen beneath Triton's surface. If the liquid reaches the supercold surface, it flash-freezes into an umbrella-shaped ice geyser, a jet of ice crystals and dark material up to five miles (eight kilometers) high. Caught in the gentle breezes of Triton's thin atmosphere, the plume falls to the surface in windblown streaks.

Looking back toward the warmth of the inner solar system, an imaginary future space probe passes Pluto and its moon, Charon. Distant Pluto remains the only planet we have not seen up close.

Pluto: At the Edge of Night

Pluto is the smallest, coldest, and most distant planet in the solar system. Discovered in 1930, it remains the only planet found in the twentieth century and the only one never visited by spacecraft from Earth.

American Clyde Tombaugh found the tiny world after months of scanning photographs of the sky. Its moon, Charon, was found in 1978. Half the size of Pluto itself, Charon circles the planet every 6.4 days. Both were named for inhabitants of the dark underworld in Greek mythology.

Pluto circles the Sun in the strangest path of any planet, taking nearly 250 years to make one complete orbit. From 1979 to 1999, it's actually closer to the Sun than Neptune.

Pluto Charon

11,800 miles (18,880 km)

Earth

Moon

238,000 miles (380,800 km)

Pluto and Earth share one thing in common—their moons are unusually large when compared to the planets themselves. Pluto and Earth are often called "double planets".

  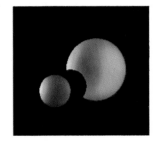

Every 125 years, Pluto and its moon eclipse each other as seen from Earth. This eclipse cycle lasts about six years, with eclipses occuring every few days. Charon eclipses Pluto in the maps above.

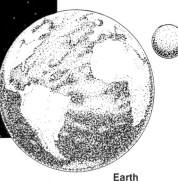

Pluto

Pluto is an icy world only one-fifth the size of Earth. It is the solar system's smallest planet.

Earth

The huge tilt of Pluto's orbit—17°, the largest of any planet—keeps Neptune and Pluto from colliding. It is as warm now on Pluto as it ever gets, about –369° F (–223° C). This heat wave turns surface ice into a gas and gives little Pluto a thin atmosphere.

From Pluto, the Sun is just the brightest of countless stars in a black sky. Frozen gases like methane and nitrogen form a brittle, icy landscape. Together, Pluto and Charon share the frigid darkness, the farthest worlds known.

Facts About Pluto

Discovered:
1930, by Clyde Tombaugh

Diameter:
1,416 miles (2,280 km), or 18% that of Earth

Surface Temperature:
–369° F, (–223°C)

Atmosphere:
Extremely thin, contains methane

Length of Day:
6 days, 9 hours, 17 minutes
Planet spins opposite to rotation of Earth

Satellites:
1

Satellite Data

Name	Diameter	Discovered
Charon	721 miles (1,160 km)	1978

Length of Year:
248 years, 182 days

Distance from Sun:
3,666,347,000 miles (5,900,140,000 km), or 39.4 times that of Earth

Pluto

Comet West, which appeared in 1976, was one of the brightest comets of recent times. Its two tails show up clearly in this photograph: a straight, bluish tail of glowing gas and a broad, yellowish fan of dust particles.

Comets: Vagabonds of the Solar System

Comets are the most distant members of the solar system and the least predictable. A bright comet seems to come out of nowhere, its long tail stretching across the night sky for weeks, then disappears just as quickly as it heads back into the cold depths of space. Such comets may not be seen again for millions of years, if at all.

Comets have long had a bad reputation. Ancient people thought they were warning signs from the gods. Some people imagined that the comet's long tail resembled a knife or a sword and foretold of new wars. Others believed that the comet brought disease and famine. For all the trouble comets were thought to bring, their name seems innocent enough. It comes from a Greek word meaning "long-haired star".

The first to predict the sighting of a comet was English astronomer Edmond Halley. In

Famous Comets

Name	Last Seen	Notes
Encke	Always visible through telescopes	Faint comet with shortest orbit known, just 3.3 years to circle sun.
Halley	1986	First comet whose return was predicted (1695, by Edmond Halley); circles Sun every 76 years, due to return in 2061; first comet whose nucleus was studied up close by space probes (1986); observed as early as 240 B.C.
IRAS-Araki-Alcock	1983	First comet named for a satellite (IRAS); passed within 2.8 million miles (4.5 million km) of Earth, second closest comet on record; may never return.
West	1976	Brilliant comet; astronomers watched the nucleus break up as it neared the Sun; not due back for thousands of years.

Comet Ikeya-Seki thrilled astronomers in 1965 by skimming the Sun's surface. It missed the Sun by only 725,000 miles (1.2 million kilometers).

1695, while collecting comet observations for a new book, Halley noticed that several comets traveled in similar paths. Halley believed that the bright comets seen in 1531, 1607, and 1682 were actually one comet that returned to the Earth's neighborhood every seventy-six years or so. He predicted—correctly—that the comet would again return in 1758. It has carried Halley's name ever since, although comets are usually named for the people who first sight them. By examining historical records, astronomers have found notations for sightings of Comet Halley for every return since 240 B.C.

Astronomers classify comets into two groups according to the time they take to circle the Sun. Comets that complete an orbit in 200 years or less are called periodic comets, while those that take longer are called long-period comets. The comet with the shortest known orbit circles the Sun in just 3.3 years.

All comets once moved in long-period orbits. Those now in periodic orbits were captured by the planets Jupiter and Saturn. When a comet passes close to either of these giants, the strong gravity may force it into a smaller periodic orbit or kick it out of the solar system entirely.

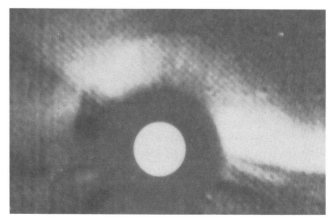

In 1979, a satellite captured the fall of a comet into the Sun (represented by the white disk). The comet nears the Sun (left) and breaks apart. Dust from the dead comet's tail makes it around the Sun (right).

An artist's impression of the great meteor shower of 1833, seen from Niagara Falls in New York. The dusty debris from a comet created the show.

Like asteroids, comets are pieces of interplanetary rubble remaining from the formation of the planets. The difference is that comets formed in the outermost fringes of the solar system, far away from the warmth of the young Sun. The solid part of a comet is called its *nucleus*. The nucleus is too small to see even with the largest of telescopes, usually between one and thirty miles (two and fifty kilometers) across. Astronomers describe a comet's nucleus as a dirty snowball, a body made up of frozen water coated with dark dust.

As a comet moves toward the inner solar system, the dark nucleus undergoes an incredible change. The Sun warms it, turning exposed icy surfaces directly into a gas. The jets become stronger as the comet nears the Sun, the dark crust cracks and exposes more ice. A growing cloud of gas and dust completely hides the nucleus.

Sunlight excites the gas and it glows with a faint bluish light. A thin stream of gas rushing away from the Sun pushes back the comet's gas cloud, forming one part of the tail. Dust particles take a slightly different route, fanning out along the comet's orbit. They reflect light from the Sun, so the comet's dust tail glows with a yellow light. If the comet's path brushes the Earth's, the dust particles

Warmed by the Sun, an exposed patch of ice boils away on a comet nucleus. The gas jets wear away the surface and carry off small particles, littering the comet's path with dusty debris.

create a meteor shower when they run into the atmosphere.

In 1986, space probes gave astronomers the opportunity to view a comet up close. One probe, named *Giotto*, passed within 375 miles (600 kilometers) of Comet Halley's nucleus. The photographs it sent back show violent jets of gas and dust erupting from a dark potato-shaped nucleus just nine miles (fifteen kilometers) long and five miles (eight kilometers) wide.

Comets wear out a little with each appearance and eventually must fade away. Astronomers discover several new comets each year, and they believe that millions circle the Sun in a comet cloud some thousands of times more distant than Pluto. Only the feeble gravity of a passing star is needed to start new comets on their long fall toward the Sun.

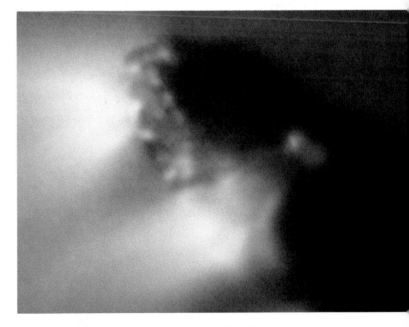

The core of Comet Halley as seen from the Giotto space probe in 1986. Several bright jets erupt from the dark nucleus.

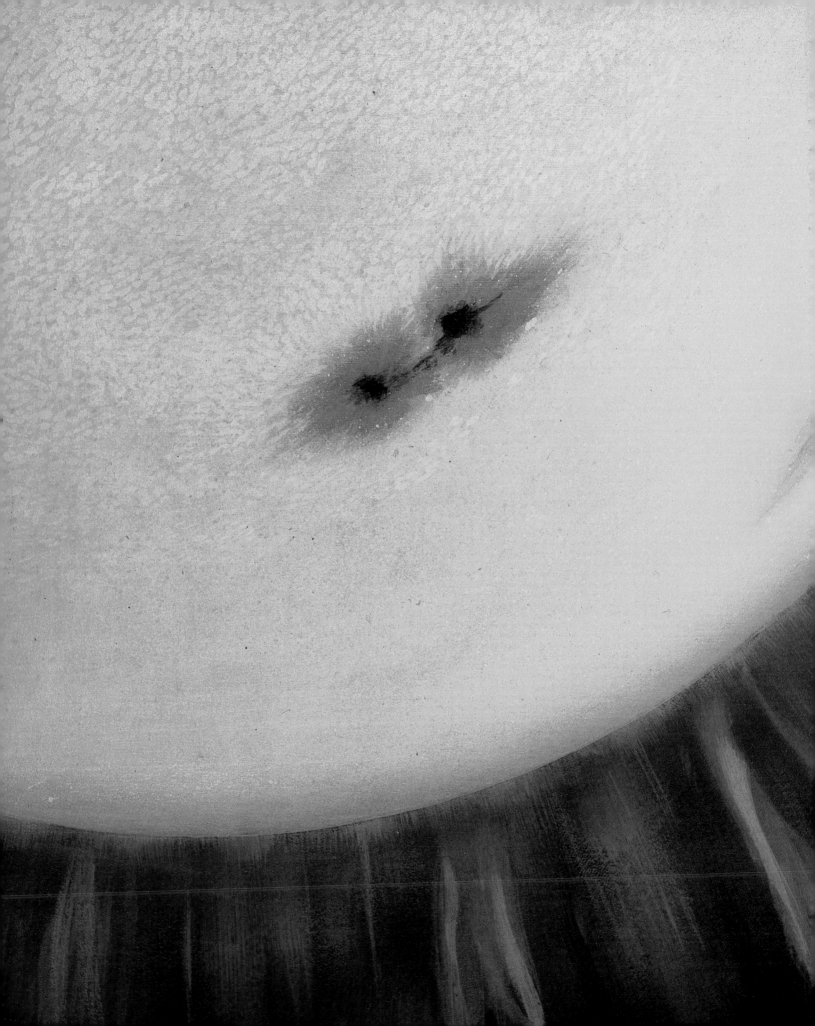

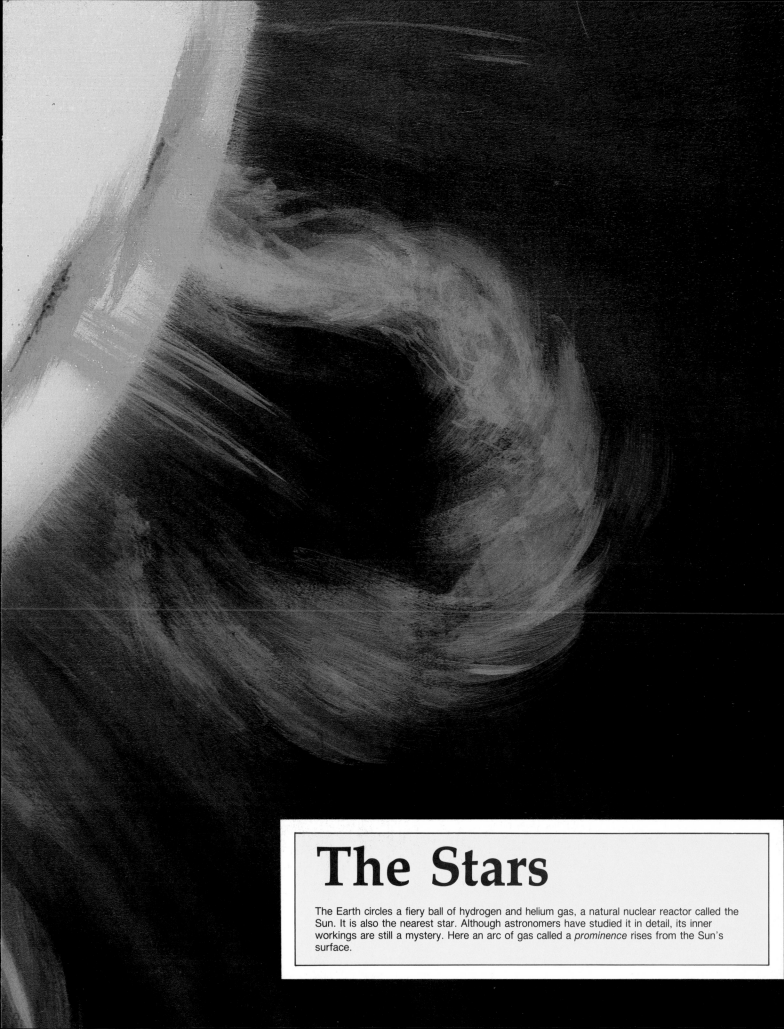

The Stars

The Earth circles a fiery ball of hydrogen and helium gas, a natural nuclear reactor called the Sun. It is also the nearest star. Although astronomers have studied it in detail, its inner workings are still a mystery. Here an arc of gas called a *prominence* rises from the Sun's surface.

The Sun: The Nearest Star

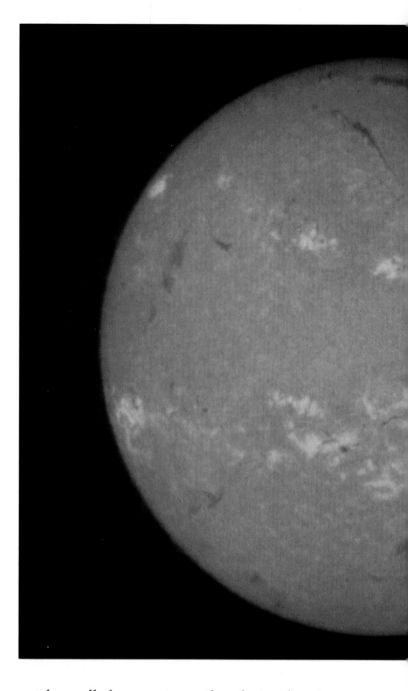

The Sun is the star around which Earth and the other planets revolve. It is the largest body in the solar system, some 750 times more massive than the combined bulk of all other objects. It is Earth's source of light and heat. It is, quite simply, the nearest star.

The Sun is an enormous ball of hydrogen and helium gas some 865,000 miles (1.4 million kilometers) across, or nearly 110 times Earth's size. Because the Sun is made of gas, different parts rotate at different speeds. At the equator, the Sun takes about twenty-four days to make one complete spin. The Sun's visible surface, called the *photosphere*, has a temperature of 10,300° F (5,700° C). The gases heat up and become more compressed at deeper levels, until the temperature reaches 27 million° F (15 million° C) deep within the Sun's energy-producing core.

The planets are actually immersed in the outermost part of the Sun. Called the *solar wind*, it is a thin stream of electrically charged particles that flows out from the Sun and fills the space between the planets. The solar wind pushes back the glowing gases of a comet to create the comet's tail.

The solar wind is really an extension of the Sun's hot outer atmosphere, called the *corona*. It stretches millions of miles above the solar surface. During a total solar eclipse, the corona appears as a strange milky glow around the Sun's darkened disk.

The Sun's photosphere is only about 250 miles (400 kilometers) deep, but it is a swirling, explosive mass of hot gases and powerful magnetic fields. Dark, mottled patches called *sunspots* are the photosphere's most familiar features. First observed by the Italian astronomer Galileo Galilei in 1610, sunspots are pockets of cooler gas sometimes half the temperature of surrounding regions. Over 200 years later, a German amateur astronomer named Samuel Heinrich Schwabe discovered that the number of sunspots increases and decreases in an orderly eleven-year cycle. The greater the number of sunspots, the greater the potential for violent behavior from the Sun.

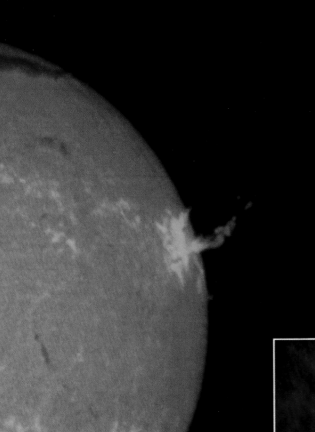

Facts About the Sun

Diameter:
865,000 miles (1,392,000 km), or
109 times that of Earth

Mass:
333,000 times that of Earth

Surface Temperature:
10,300° F (5,700° C)

Central Temperature:
27 million° F (15 million° C)

Composition:
70% hydrogen, 27% helium

Spin (at equator):
26 days, 21 hours

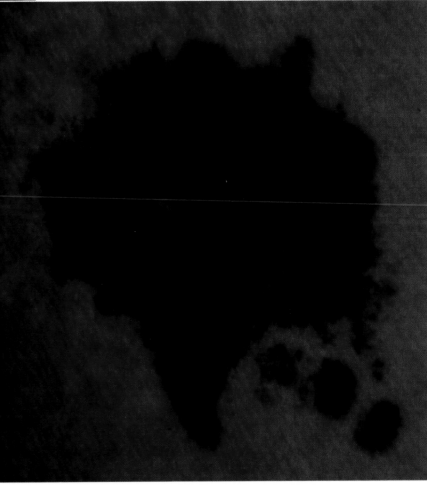

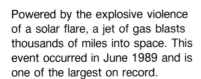

Powered by the explosive violence
of a solar flare, a jet of gas blasts
thousands of miles into space. This
event occurred in June 1989 and is
one of the largest on record.

Sunspots are disturbed areas on the Sun's surface. This group, which appeared in
March 1989, produced intense flares for two weeks. The cluster of spots is many
times larger than Earth.

Sunspots contain intense magnetic fields that can trigger violent eruptions. These outbursts, called *flares,* are sudden energy releases that usually last no more than an hour. The energy released in one hour by a large flare could power a major city for 200 million years. The blast from a large flare includes x-rays, ultraviolet and visible light, and waves of subatomic particles. These can damage satellites, interrupt radio and TV signals, and create beautiful skyglows called the *aurora.* The aurora occurs when fast-moving particles strike atoms in Earth's atmosphere, setting them aglow.

Arcs of gas rise high above the Sun's photosphere and sometimes eject material into the corona. They are called *prominences* when seen as bright arches at the Sun's edge, or *filaments* when seen as cool, dark threads on the bright solar disk.

A nuclear reaction occurring in the high-temperature core fuels all of the Sun's activity. The reaction is called nuclear *fusion.* In this process, the nuclei of hydrogen atoms smash into one another and join, eventually forming a helium nucleus and giving off energy. Each second, the Sun converts 584 million tons of hydrogen into 580 million tons of helium. The remaining four million tons is converted directly into high-energy radiation. Astronomers believe the Sun to be an average-size, middle-aged star. At its current energy output, the Sun's hydrogen fuel will last another five billion years.

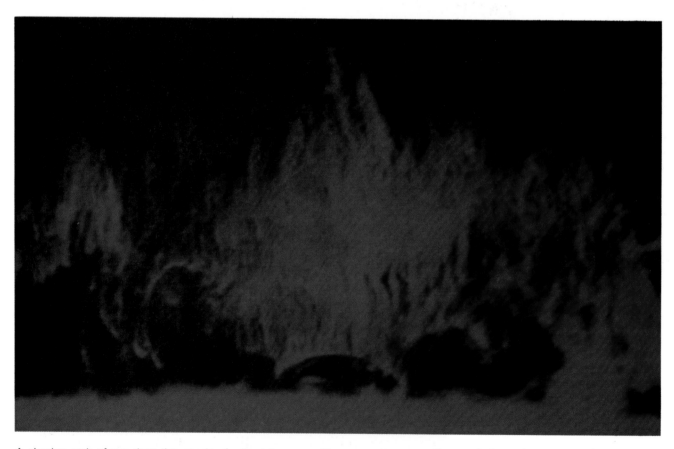

A glowing arch of gas rises thousands of miles into space. These enormous eruptions, called prominences, can be seen stretching into space along the edge of the Sun. Violent prominences rise at speeds of up to 125 miles (200 kilometers) per second.

A total solar eclipse occurs when the Moon passes precisely between Earth and the Sun. For a few minutes, while the Moon blocks the brilliant solar disk, the delicate structure of the Sun's faint outer atmosphere, the corona, can be observed.

A solar eclipse occurs when Earth passes through the Moon's shadow. In a lunar eclipse, the Moon passes into the shadow cast by Earth. A solar eclipse can occur only at new moon, a lunar eclipse at full moon.

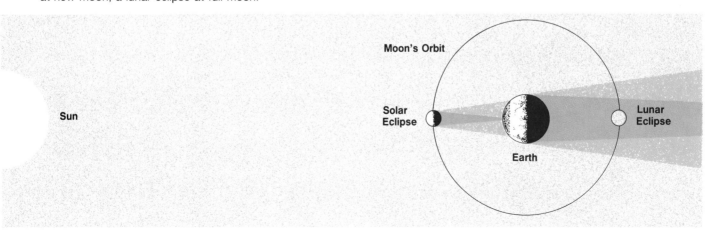

Sun

Moon's Orbit

Solar Eclipse

Lunar Eclipse

Earth

Star Birth, Star Death

The very beginning of a star's life is hidden from the view of telescopes. Until recently, astronomers could only guess at the conditions attending the birth of a star. Modern instruments, particularly heat-sensitive telescopes in orbit above Earth, have permitted scientists to peer into the cool, dark, dust clouds where all stars are born.

About five billion years ago, the Sun began its life deep within the darkness of a giant cloud of gas and dust, or *nebula.* Perhaps triggered by the shock wave of an exploding star,

part of the cloud became compressed. More gas and dust joined this cloud, and soon gravity pulled it even closer together. This loose ball of gas and dust kept contracting, heating up as it shrank and spinning ever faster. Deep within the cloud, or protosun, temperatures and densities soared to a critical point. The protostar's internal furnace was lit—hydrogen fused into helium and energy. The protosun became a star.

The outer portions of the cloud that formed the Sun became flattened by its rapid rota-

Glowing with the light of newborn stars, the Great Nebula in Orion marks the site of a vast stellar nursery. Behind this glowing veil lies the dark cloud where star birth occurs.

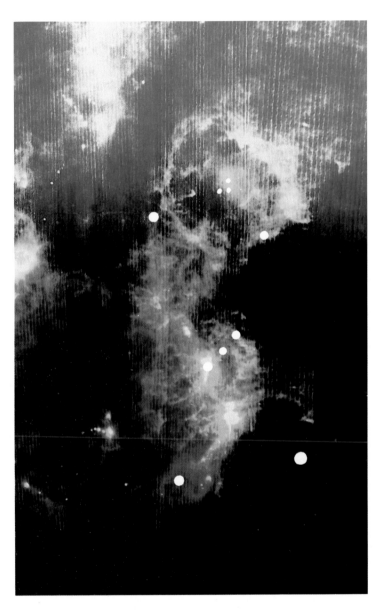

Star-forming regions in the constellation Orion show up as red areas in this map made by a heat-sensitive telescope. The white dots show the location of bright stars.

tion. Dust particles collided, stuck together, and collided again to make the building blocks of the planets. When the Sun ignited its internal fires, powerful flares and a violent solar wind swept much of the gas out of the inner solar system. Rocky bodies formed near the Sun, and planets that were giant balls of gas condensed farther out.

The Sun has brightened somewhat since its early days. Its rotation has slowed, its violent flares have settled down, and its activity follows a steady eleven-year cycle. Not much will change for the next five billion years.

Every star wages a battle with gravity. Gravity tries to compress the star still further, but the energy-producing reactions within the star's core generate a balancing pressure. In about five billion years, the Sun will begin to lose its battle.

The Sun's energy crisis will begin as it exhausts the fuel in its core. Over a period of two billion years, the Sun's fires will wane slightly. Gravity will pull inward, and the Sun will contract and heat up. It will begin using hydrogen fuel lying outside of its core.

Now at a higher temperature, the Sun will expand a little.

This process will continue until the Sun has expanded to 100 times its present size. It will balloon to beyond the orbit of Mercury, incinerating its innermost planets. Earth's seas and atmosphere will have evaporated long ago. The Sun's inflated red disk will fill the sky. Earth's surface, now as hot as 2,600°F (1,430° C), will be a sea of molten rock. The Sun will become a *red giant*.

The Sun's red giant stage will last only 250 million years. Another energy crisis will force it to contract and heat up. This time the temperature within the Sun will soar to the point where the helium in its core undergoes fusion, turning into heavier elements and releasing energy. When this new energy source turns on, violent shock waves will ripple through the Sun.

The first direct photograph of a cloud of dust around another star reveals a bright disk of dust around the star Beta Pictoris. As shown in the painting, rocky fragments and possibly even planets may inhabit the disk.

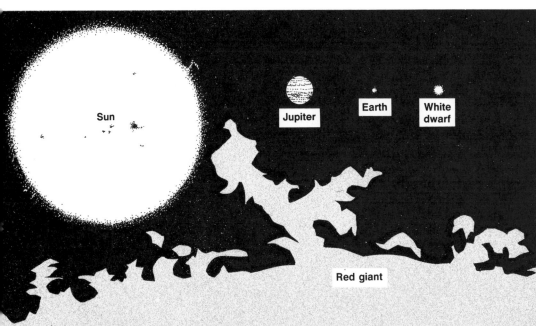

Sun

Jupiter

Earth

White dwarf

Red giant

The Sun's life began when it formed over 4.5 billion years ago. In another five billion years, it will redden and swell to 100 times its present size, swallowing the planets Mercury and Venus. It will then cast off its outer layers and become a tiny white dwarf.

This painting shows the progression of the Sun throughout its life. Its size changes dramatically as it ages, first ballooning to a red giant, then shrinking to a planet-sized white dwarf.

The wreckage of an exploded star, the Crab Nebula contains a superdense neutron star spinning thirty times a second. Because this neutron star emits pulses of light and radio waves, it is called a *pulsar*.

Pueblo Indian carvings in Arizona caves may record the sudden appearance of a supernova (left) near the crescent moon (right) on the morning of July 5, 1054. This exploding star created the Crab Nebula.

Eventually the Sun will settle into a new routine. The vast energy from the core will slowly blow off the outer layers of its atmosphere until the core itself is revealed. About half the Sun's mass will be crammed into a hot, Earth-sized ball. The Sun will become a *white dwarf.*

As a white dwarf, the Sun's light will be a thousand times weaker than it is today. Its intense ultraviolet light sets the expanding atmosphere aglow, creating a bright bubble around what is left of the solar system. At the age of fifteen billion years, the Sun will slowly cool and fade for several billion years. Then the planets will circle a black, burned-out cinder.

There are worse ways for a star to go. Those much larger than the Sun experience a

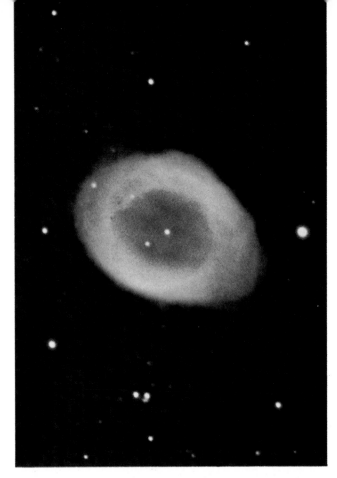

Some twenty thousand years ago, a star blew off its outer layers and created this expanding shell of gas. Ultraviolet light from the central star sets the gas aglow.

The violent explosion of a supernova (above white line) lets one star briefly outshine all the others in the galaxy. This supernova occurred in galaxy NGC 4725 in 1941.

far more violent end. Near the end of its life, such a star contains layers in which hydrogen, helium, carbon, and other elements undergo nuclear fusion. Still, the star reaches a point where even these reactions can no longer support the crushing weight of its outer layers. In a second the star's innermost regions collapse, triggering an explosion that blasts the star apart. This explosion is called a *supernova.*

Although as many as three supernovas may occur in Earth's galaxy each century, none have been seen for more than three hundred years. No one knows when the next one will appear, but the Milky Way is overdue. In 1987, a supernova exploded in a small nearby galaxy known as the Large Magellanic Cloud. Even from this great distance, the star briefly became as bright as some of the brightest in the sky. As the shell of gas blown off the star dispersed, the supernova faded from view.

Supernovas may also leave behind a small, dense object called a *neutron star* or even a *black hole,* from which even light cannot escape. Supernova blasts spread the chemicals forged within stars out into space. They are believed to be the sources of the heavy elements from which both Earth and its inhabitants are made.

The Galaxy and Beyond

While Earth's galaxy can only be seen from within, its appearance to an intergalactic traveler can be imagined. Older, redder stars make up the dense central core of the Milky Way Galaxy. Bright blue stars color the spiral arms. These are stellar nurseries rich in the gas and dust from which new stars are born.

The Milky Way

The Milky Way is the name of a hazy band that encircles the sky, the combined light of many distant stars. This view shows the thickest part of the Milky Way, the vast star clouds near the constellation Sagittarius. The center of the galaxy lies about twenty-eight thousand light-years in this direction.

The Milky Way is a softly glowing band that winds its way along the night sky. It is the combined light of billions of stars so far away they cannot be seen individually. It is our view, from the inside out, of our own galaxy. Because of this, Earth's galaxy is often called the Milky Way.

The glow of the Milky Way forms a band because the galaxy is flattened into a disk. The glow is brighter in one direction, toward the constellation Sagittarius, because in that direction lies the very center of the galaxy. The actual center cannot be seen because clouds of dust block it from view.

The scale of the galaxy is far beyond that of the solar system. Miles or kilometers may work for stating the distances to planets, but they are much too small to deal with the vast distances within the Milky Way. Instead, astronomers use a measurement based on the speed of light. Light travels through space at a speed of 186,282 miles (299,792 kilometers) per second. In one year, light tracks 5.88 trillion miles (9.5 trillion kilometers). This distance is called the *light-year*.

The galaxy is a roughly spherical ball of older, redder stars set within a flat disk of gas and dust about 100,000 light-years across and thirteen hundred light-years thick. Within the disk, bright, blue, young stars light up the gas clouds that formed them. Seen from outside the galaxy, these highlights in the

Facts About the Milky Way Galaxy

Diameter:	Mass:	Distance between spiral arms:	Thickness of galactic disk:	Satellite galaxies:
100,000 light-years	About 200 billion suns	6,500 light-years	1,300 light-years	2 (visible only in the southern sky)

Satellite Data

Name	Mass	Diameter	Distance
Large Magellanic Cloud	10 billion suns	40,000 light-years	173,000 light-years
Small Magellanic Cloud	1 billion suns	30,000 light-years	225,000 light-years

The brightly glowing gas of the Lagoon Nebula, about thirty-three hundred light-years off, mark it as a site where stars are being born.

disk create a set of spiral arms that wind outward from the central regions. The Sun lies within such a spiral arm about twenty-eight thousand light-years from the galactic center. It takes 200 million years for the solar system to orbit once around the galaxy.

Stars are not the only components of the galaxy. Great clouds of gas and dust are the factories where new stars are built. Usually, stars form in groups called *open clusters.* These loose stellar associations are called open because the stars within them gradually drift apart as they age. Member stars wander off under the gentle tugs of the gravity of other stars. The Sun probably was born within such a grouping.

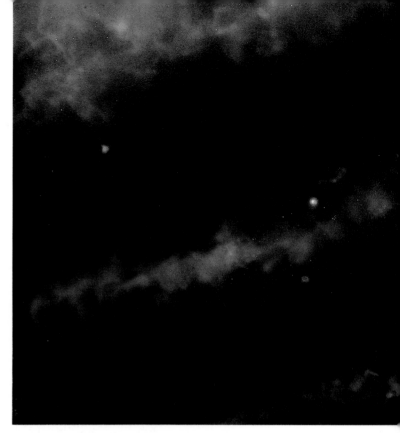

This painting shows the spiral arms nearest the solar system. The Perseus arm, at top, is some sixty-five hundred light-years away. The Sagittarius arm, at bottom, lies about sixty-five hundred light-years toward the center. The Sun is within the Orion arm, at center.

Top: Stars in the young open cluster known as NGC 3293, some ten thousand light-years away, will drift farther and farther apart as the cluster ages.

Bottom: This vast ball of stars, named NGC 104, lies some sixteen thousand light-years away. Gravity holds the stars together. Containing perhaps a million stars, globular clusters circle the galaxy in distant, lazy orbits.

Another type of star cluster orbits the perimeter of the galaxy. They look like great balls of stars, which is exactly what they are. A hundred thousand to perhaps a million stars crowd into a sphere just a few hundred light-years across. These objects are called *globular clusters.* They contain some of the oldest stars of the galaxy and probably formed before it flattened into a disk. The orbits of globular clusters usually keep them far from the galaxy's gas-rich disk. Some of the most distant may take billions of years to complete one circuit.

Still farther out orbit a pair of small, oddly-shaped galaxies called the Large and Small Magellanic Clouds. They were first reported to European astronomers by the first explorers to sail around the world. Led by Portuguese nobleman Ferdinand Magellan in 1519, the expedition sailed into southern seas. There the crew saw stars not visible from their home port. The galaxies were given their cumbersome names in honor of Magellan, who was killed during the trip.

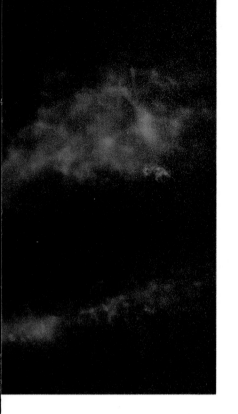

The Milky Way is a normal spiral galaxy about 100,000 light-years in diameter. It is centered on a compact central region surrounded by a cloud of stars called the central bulge. The flattened disk holds most of the galaxy's gas and dust. The spiral arms represent portions of the disk made visible by hot, young stars. A halo of globular clusters surrounds the galaxy.

Galactic Neighbors

The closest galaxy like the Milky Way is the spiral in the constellation Andromeda, about 2.2 million light-years distant. This galaxy is flanked by a pair of small satellite galaxies. The stars scattered across the picture all belong to the Milky Way.

During the nineteenth century, astronomers found that some of the cloud-like patches of light called *nebulae* had a spiral shape to them. Many astronomers believed that these spiral nebulae were nothing special, just vast swirling clouds of gas and dust within the Milky Way Galaxy. Others suggested the spirals were island universes, or whole galaxies like the Milky Way, so far away that the stars within them could not be clearly seen.

The scientific argument about the nature of spiral nebulae continued into this century. Were the spirals small nearby gas clouds or enormous far-off collections of stars? Since there was no reliable way of measuring the distances to these objects, the argument could not be settled one way or the other.

A variable star provided the key. Variable stars change in brightness, often in a fixed cycle. In 1912, astronomers noticed that one type of variable star showed a relationship between its brightness and the length of its cycle. Astronomers could figure the distance to these stars just by measuring the length of time in which they brighten, fade, and brighten again.

In 1923, American astronomer Edwin

The Large Magellanic Cloud, a satellite of the Milky Way, is an unorganized collection of stars and gas.

The monster galaxy known as M87 contains some three thousand billion stars, enough to make dozens of Milky Way galaxies. The small fuzzy "stars" surrounding M87 are actually some of its ten thousand globular clusters.

Hubble discovered the same type of star in the bright spiral nebula in Andromeda known as M31. The distance Hubble calculated from observations of variable stars placed them millions of light-years away. This was far beyond the boundaries of the Milky Way. The spiral nebulae were truly distant galaxies.

Most large galaxies are spirals like the Milky Way. Their bulging central regions are filled with older, redder stars and lack the fresh gas and dust to make new ones. Gas and dust enriches their flattened disks, and bright patches of hot, young stars create the appearance of uncoiling spiral arms.

The arms of a spiral do not rotate in one piece. Their inner parts circle the galaxy faster than their ends. These stretch and shear the arms until they fade away. Before this occurs, new star-forming regions brighten to create highlights that preserve the spiral pattern.

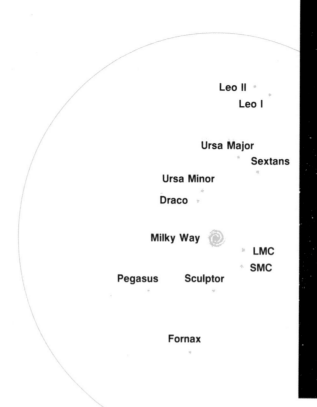

Andromeda Galaxy

Leo II

Leo I

Ursa Major

Sextans

Ursa Minor

Draco

Milky Way

LMC

SMC

Pegasus   Sculptor

Fornax

This map shows the nearby galactic neighborhood, called the Local Group. The circles mark intervals of one million light-years. The Milky Way and Andromeda spirals are the group's two largest masses.

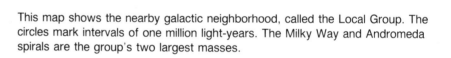

Another type of galaxy, called *elliptical*, looks very different from the colorful spirals. Ellipticals are nearly spherical objects composed of billions of aged, reddened stars. Almost no gas and dust remains within them—they have long ago exhausted their ability to make new stars. Ellipticals range in size from tiny dwarf galaxies with only a few million stars to vast star piles like M87, a mass of thousands of billions of stars.

The last major form of galaxy is called *irregular*. These galaxies have neither the simple structure of ellipticals nor the complex patterns of spirals. They are disorganized collections of gas, dust, and stars. Many irregulars orbit around larger galaxies. The Magellanic Clouds, small satellites that orbit the Milky Way Galaxy, are good examples of irregular galaxies. The intense gravity of the galaxies they circle may keep them in disarray.

Some galaxies show signs of more direct interaction with their satellites or neighbors. The distorted spiral arms of galaxy M51 result from a near collision with a passing galaxy. The thick, warped disk and intense radio and x-ray emissions from NGC 5128 suggest that it collided with and consumed a small spiral galaxy.

The gravity of galaxies also holds them together. Within three million light-years of the Milky Way there lies about two dozen galaxies of all shapes and sizes. The Milky Way and M31 represent the main bulk of this cluster, called the Local Group.

This loose spiral, called M33, holds only about 10 percent of the Milky Way's mass. A member of the Local Group, it lies some 2.6 million light-years away.

Its disk partly hidden by a band of obscuring dust, the giant galaxy NGC 5128 contains perhaps three hundred billion stars. It may be the end product of a galactic collision.

M51 is a classic spiral galaxy. Arms rich in gas, dust, and newborn stars uncoil from its center.

The Distant Universe

The Local Group, the small cluster of galaxies that includes the Milky Way, is small and loosely packed. Beyond it astronomers recognize dozens of other clusters of galaxies. Some, like the Coma cluster, contain many elliptical galaxies. Others hold many gas-rich spirals like the Milky Way. The Virgo cluster, just seventy million light-years distant, is an example. Of the twenty-five hundred galaxies observed within it, nearly two thousand are spirals.

Galaxies cluster together because they interact with one another's gravity. The Milky Way and the Andromeda galaxy, for example, orbit about their common center of gravity within the Local Group. Smaller galaxies move around the larger ones.

The great Virgo cluster is really the central part of the Local Supercluster, an assembly of galaxy clusters that includes the Local Group. Gravity holds clusters together, but superclusters must slowly spread in different directions. Still, they are the largest structures scientists know of, stretching up to 300 million light-years across.

The farthest objects astronomers have found are the quasars. They look like blue-white stars—in fact, their name means "star-

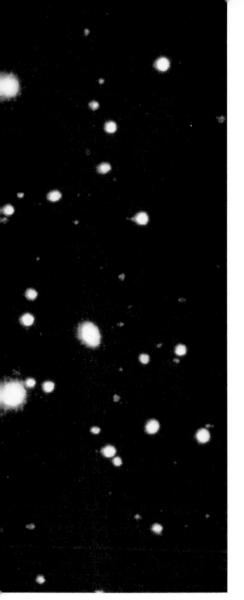

Two enormous elliptical galaxies (center) orbit one another in the heart of the Coma cluster of galaxies, some 500 million light-years away. About thirteen hundred large galaxies (yellow disks) can be found in this densely packed cluster.

Quasars appear to be extremely brilliant galactic centers, possibly galaxies like the Milky Way in the first stages of formation. In this painting, the galaxy's spiral arms are almost lost in the glare of its brilliant, exploding core.

like." But quasars emit far more energy than hundreds of giant galaxies. The incredible amount of energy they release makes them detectable across billions of light-years. No one knows what fuels these mysterious objects. They are the beacons of the distant cosmos. First discovered in 1963, over six hundred quasars are now known. The farthest quasars are more than ten billion light-years away. They were shining even as our own galaxy was taking shape, and so quasars represent a glimpse of the distant past. Quasars may be bright cores of young galaxies undergoing a violent stage of formation.

The View from Earth

Warm evenings and the bright Milky Way highlight this midsummer star party. The constellation of Scorpius the Scorpion rides high above the southern horizon. The Milky Way's faint glow is the combined light of billions of stars too far away to see.

It is convenient for astronomers to imagine the Earth as sitting inside a giant, star-studded ball called the *celestial sphere*. They can then locate objects with a variation of the latitude and longitude grid used by earthly mapmakers.

Understanding the Night Sky

The night sky is constantly changing. The Moon appears further eastward each day, its face changing as it runs through its monthly cycle of phases. Meteors occasionally streak across the sky. The five planets visible to the unaided eye—Mercury, Venus, Mars, Jupiter, and Saturn—slowly shuffle their places in the sky as they orbit the Sun.

To find their way around the sky, astronomers picture the Earth as though it sits within an even bigger ball called the *celestial sphere.*

Mapmakers identify points on the Earth by using an imaginary grid of latitude and longitude. Astronomers use the same idea to locate objects on the celestial sphere.

When the Sun rises, people speak as though the Sun is really doing something. In fact, the spin of the Earth is bringing the Sun into view. Still, it is helpful to think that the Sun, Moon, planets, and stars are attached to the sky and that the celestial sphere is spinning slowly overhead. Stars rise in the east,

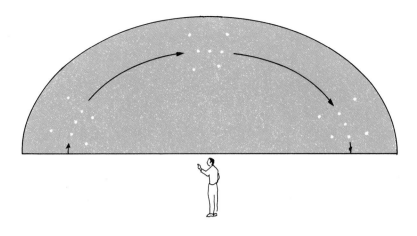

The Sun, Moon, planets, and stars rise in the east and set in the west. It is helpful to picture the sky as a great dome. As Earth rotates eastward, the dome of the sky seems to spin slowly westward, bringing new objects into view.

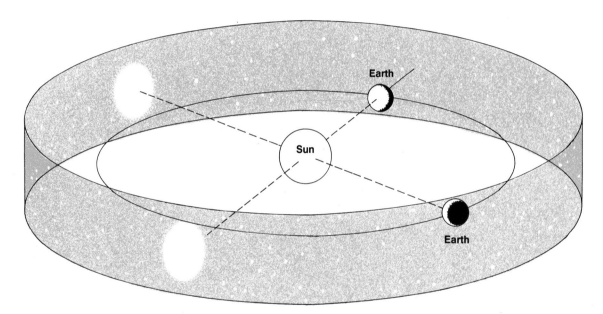

As Earth circles the Sun, its night side faces different stars. The day side faces the Sun. The white patches on the band of the sky represent stars washed out by the Sun's light.

arc high into the sky, then set in the west.

The Earth does not just spin on its axis. It also circles the Sun once a year. Stars cannot be seen during the day because of the brightness of the Sun. But as Earth makes its way around, the stars that cannot be seen by day eventually appear at night. The stars rise about four minutes earlier each day, a direct result of the Earth's orbital motion.

Constellations are patterns formed by the brightest stars in the sky. Ancient people invented these patterns and made up stories about them. Star maps are designed to help sky watchers find the brightest constellations. There is a map for each season, and each map lists the date and time it should be used. The circular border of the star maps represents the horizon, and the directions *north*, *south*, *east*, and *west* are labeled along it. Think of the sky as a great dome with its highest point overhead. The center of each star map is the overhead point.

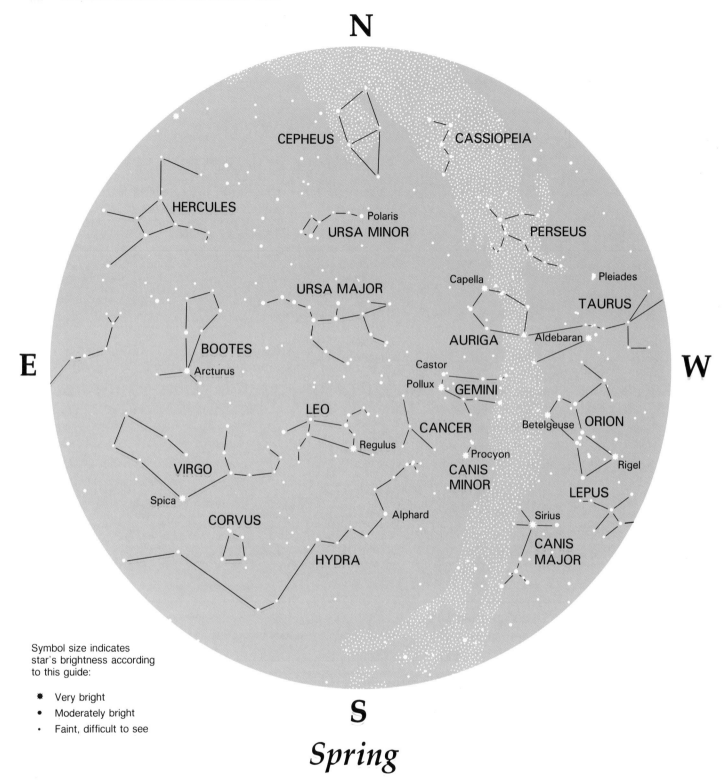

Symbol size indicates
star's brightness according
to this guide:

*   Very bright
•   Moderately bright
·   Faint, difficult to see

Spring

As the sky darkens, the bright winter constellations hang low over the western horizon. High in the south lies Leo the Lion, while Virgo the Maiden lies to the southeast. Ursa Major the Great Bear, now high overhead in the north, is best known by the pattern of its brightest stars—the Big Dipper. The curve of the Dipper's handle leads to the bright star Arcturus in Bootes the Herdsman, then to Spica in Virgo.

The map shows the sky as it appears at 10:30 p.m. in mid-March, 9:30 p.m. (daylight savings time) in mid-April, and 7:30 p.m. in mid-May.

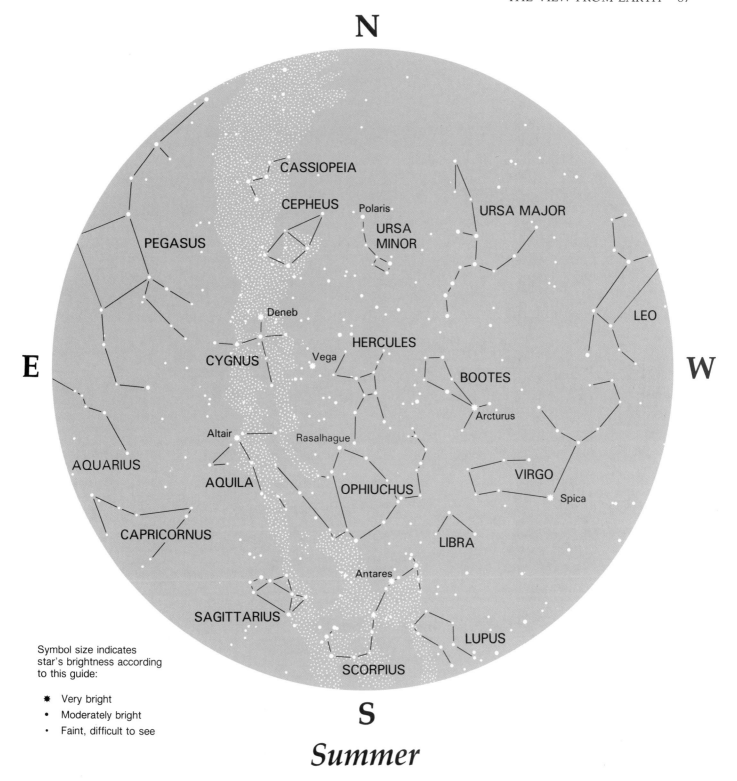

N

E

W

CASSIOPEIA

CEPHEUS

Polaris

URSA MINOR

URSA MAJOR

PEGASUS

Deneb

CYGNUS

Vega

HERCULES

BOOTES

LEO

Arcturus

Altair

Rasalhague

AQUILA

OPHIUCHUS

VIRGO

AQUARIUS

Spica

CAPRICORNUS

LIBRA

Antares

SAGITTARIUS

LUPUS

SCORPIUS

S

Symbol size indicates
star's brightness according
to this guide:

* Very bright
• Moderately bright
· Faint, difficult to see

Summer

Low in the southern sky, Scorpius the Scorpion and Sagittarius the Archer shine amidst the brightest section of the Milky Way. The very heart of the Galaxy lies twenty-eight thousand light-years in the general direction of Sagittarius. Ursa Major the Great Bear (also known as the Big Dipper) appears high in the northwest.

Cygnus the Swan and Aquila the Eagle fly high in the southeast. Bootes the Herdsman and Virgo the Maiden lie high in the southwest.

The map shows the sky as it appears at midnight in mid-June, 10:00 p.m. in mid-July, and 8:00 p.m. in mid-August.

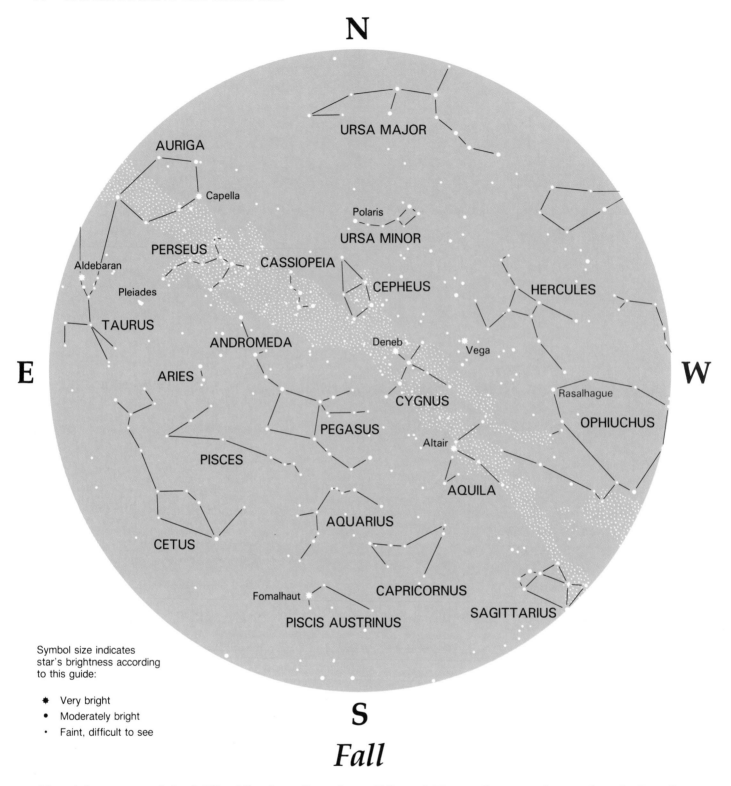

N

E

W

S

Symbol size indicates
star's brightness according
to this guide:

✴ Very bright
• Moderately bright
· Faint, difficult to see

Fall

The richest part of the Milky Way has slipped below the southwest horizon. Sagittarius the Archer is ready to follow. Its teapot-like shape is tipped as if ready to pour. High in the south, the bright stars of three constellations—Altair, Deneb, and Vega—form a pattern called the Summer Triangle. Pegasus the Winged Horse flies nearly overhead. Capella in Auriga the Charioteer leads the winter stars in the northeast.

The map shows the sky as it appears at 11:00 p.m. in mid-September, 9:00 p.m. in mid-October, and 6:00 p.m. (standard time) in mid-November.

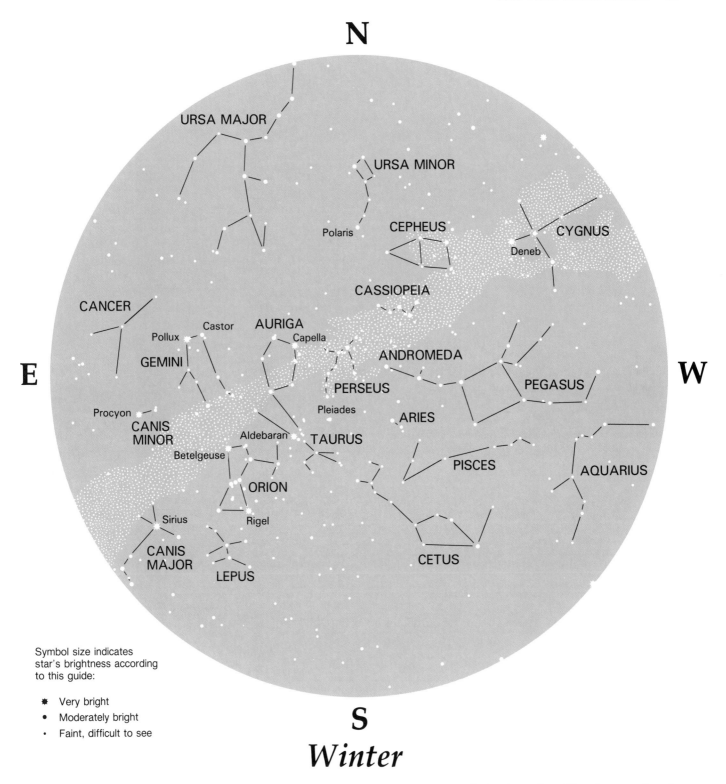

N

URSA MAJOR

URSA MINOR

Polaris

CEPHEUS

CYGNUS

Deneb

CASSIOPEIA

CANCER

AURIGA

Castor

Capella

ANDROMEDA

Pollux

GEMINI

PERSEUS

PEGASUS

Procyon

ARIES

CANIS
MINOR

Aldebaran

TAURUS

Pleiades

Betelgeuse

PISCES

AQUARIUS

ORION

Rigel

Sirius

CANIS
MAJOR

LEPUS

CETUS

E

W

Symbol size indicates
star's brightness according
to this guide:

✳ Very bright

• Moderately bright

· Faint, difficult to see

S

Winter

The great square of Pegasus the Winged Horse rides high in the western sky. Cygnus the Swan dives toward the northwest. Overhead, the W-shape of Cassiopeia the Queen makes an easy target. The most noticeable stars, however, appear high in the southeast. Orion the Hunter, Taurus the Bull, Gemini the Twins, and Auriga the Charioteer dominate the winter sky. The brightest star of all, Sirius, twinkles low in the southeast.

The map shows the sky as it appears at 10:00 p.m. in early December, 8:00 p.m. in early January, and 6:00 p.m. in early February.

Glossary

Asteroid A rocky body less than 620 miles (1,000 kilometers) across that orbits the Sun. More accurately called a *minor planet* or a *planetesimal*.

Astrology An ancient system of beliefs that attempts to explain or predict human actions by the position and interaction of the Sun, Moon, and planets. It is not a science.

Astronomy The oldest science, the study of the universe beyond Earth's atmosphere.

Axis An imaginary line passing through the center of a body, such as a planet, around which that body spins.

Black hole A collapsed object whose gravity is so strong that neither light nor matter can escape it. A black hole has never been detected with certainty, but most astronomers believe they exist.

Comet A small body made of ice and dust that orbits the Sun, usually in very elongated orbits.

Constellation One of eighty-eight areas into which astronomers divide the sky.

Core The central region of a moon, planet, or star. The energy of a star is produced in its core.

Crust The thin, outermost solid layer of a moon or terrestrial planet.

Density A measure of how tightly mass is packed into a space.

Doppler Effect A change in the frequency of sound or light waves caused by motion between the source and observer.

Eclipse The total or partial blocking of light from a celestial body caused by its passing into the shadow of another body (as in a lunar eclipse), or the hiding of one celestial body by another (as in a solar eclipse).

Ecliptic The apparent yearly path of the Sun through the sky. Since this apparent motion is actually a reflection of Earth's movement, the ecliptic also marks the plane of Earth's orbit.

Element A substance made up of the same type of atoms. Oxygen and gold are among the more than 100 known elements.

Energy The ability to do work. Motion, heat, light, and sound are all forms of energy.

Galaxy A vast collection of billions of stars, gas, and dust held together by the gravity of its members.

Gas giants The planets Jupiter, Saturn, Uranus, and Neptune.

Globular cluster A dense ball of thousands to millions of stars that orbits around a galaxy.

Gravity The force at the surface of a planet or other body that pulls mass toward its center.

Light-year The distance traveled through space by a beam of light in one year. Light travels at 186,282 miles (299,792 kilometers) per second. So, a light-year is 5.88 trillion miles (9.5 trillion kilometers), or 63,240 times Earth's distance from the Sun.

Mass The amount of matter within a body.

Matter The substance from which the universe is made. Matter exists in three familiar states: solid, liquid, and gas.

Meteor The streak of light caused by a *meteoroid* that passes through a planet's atmosphere. Also called a shooting star.

Meteorite A *meteoroid* that strikes the surface of a planet or moon.

Meteoroid A solid body in orbit about the Sun, much smaller than an asteroid and usually weighing less than about 220 pounds (100 kilograms).

Moon A natural satellite orbiting a planet. Also, the name of Earth's natural satellite.

Nebula A cloud of gas and dust, sometimes glowing from the light of nearby stars and sometimes a dark patch that blocks starlight. New stars are born within a nebula.

Neutron star The extremely dense core of a star, all that is left after a *supernova* explosion.

Nova A star that suddenly erupts, greatly increasing its brightness.

Nuclear fusion The process by which matter changes into energy and the power source for the Sun and stars. The *nuclei* of light atoms join to make heavier nuclei, releasing energy.

Nucleus Of an atom, the central portion of an atom that has a positive charge and contains most of the atom's mass. Of a comet, the solid ice-rock mixture at the center of a comet's gaseous head and tail. Of a spiral galaxy, the dense central portion made of older, redder stars (plural: nuclei).

Phases The cycle of varying shapes in the sunlit portion of a planet or moon. The Moon, Venus, and Mercury all show phases as seen from Earth.

Planet A body of substantial size held in orbit by the gravity of a star. A planet reflects the light of a nearby star.

Pressure A measure of the force exerted on a surface.

Pulsar A neutron star that rotates rapidly and emits a beam of radiation.

Quasar A "quasi-stellar," or starlike, object probably part of a galaxy's core. They are the most distant objects visible. Also known as QSOs.

Radar Radio signals transmitted to and bounced back from an object. It stands for *Ra*dio *D*etection *A*nd *R*anging.

Radiation Energy transmitted through space as waves or particles.

Satellite A natural or artificial body in orbit around a planet.

Solar wind A stream of electrically charged particles from the Sun.

Star A hot, glowing sphere of gas, usually one that emits energy from nuclear reactions in its core.

Sunspot A magnetic disturbance on the Sun. It is cooler than the surrounding area and, consequently, appears darker.

Supernova A stellar explosion that increases the brightness of the star by thousands of times.

Terrestrial planets Mercury, Venus, Earth, and Mars.

Tides Periodic changes in the shape of a planet, moon, or star caused by the gravity of a body near it.

Variable star A star whose brightness changes.

White dwarf A collapsed object formed from a star that has exhausted its nuclear fuel. The Sun will one day become a white dwarf.

Index

Numbers in *italics* refer to illustrations or maps.

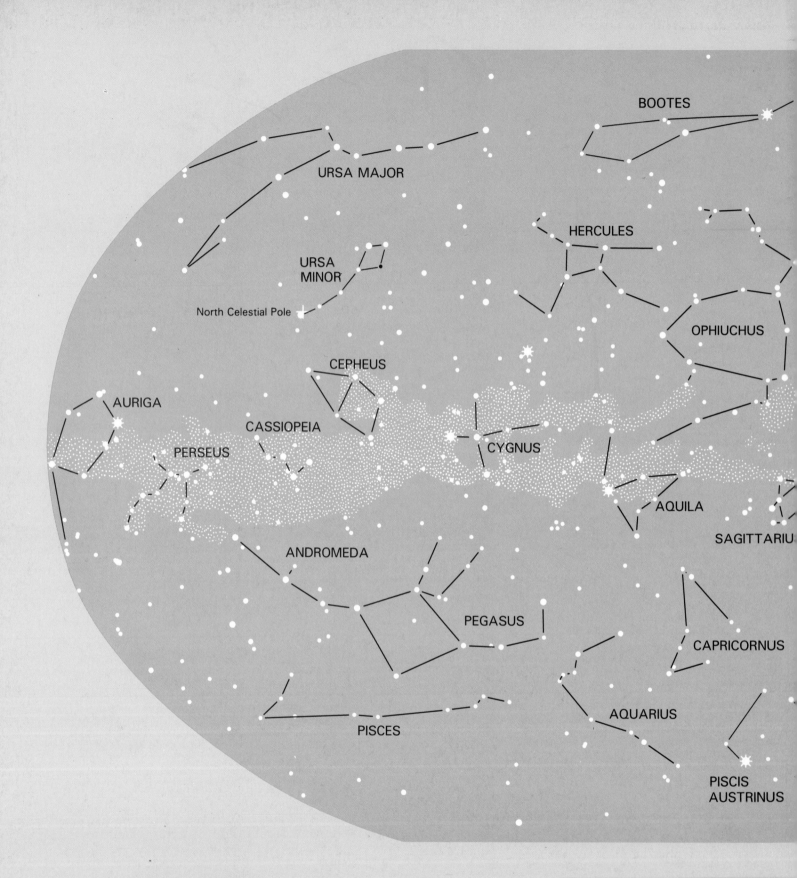

BOOTES

URSA MAJOR

HERCULES

URSA
MINOR

North Celestial Pole

OPHIUCHUS

CEPHEUS

AURIGA

CASSIOPEIA

CYGNUS

PERSEUS

AQUILA

ANDROMEDA

SAGITTARIU

PEGASUS

CAPRICORNUS

AQUARIUS

PISCES

PISCIS
AUSTRINUS

The Galaxy as
Seen From Within

Piecing together the structure of the Galaxy is a difficult task.
We view the Galaxy from the inside on a planet whose axis is
tilted with respect to the glowing band of the Milky Way, the
Galaxy's disk. This map reveals the night sky as it would